THE DECORATED GARDEN ROOM

THE DECORATED GARDEN ROOM

Interior design for your outside living space

TESSA EVELEGH

Photography by **DEBBIE PATTERSON**

LORENZ BOOKS

NEW YORK • LONDON • SYDNEY • BATH

For Jennie

This edition published in 1996 by Lorenz Books
an imprint of Anness Publishing Limited
administration office: 27 West 20th Street
New York, NY 10011

© Anness Publishing Limited 1996

Lorenz Books are available for bulk purchase for sales
promotion and for premium use. For details write or call
the manager of special sales, LORENZ BOOKS,
27 West 20th Street, New York, NY 10011; (212) 807–6739.

Produced by Anness Publishing Limited
1 Boundary Row
London SE1 8HP

ISBN 1 85967 103 9

Publisher: **Joanna Lorenz**
Project Editor: **Judith Simons**
Text Editor: **Maggie Daykin**
Designer: **Lisa Tai**
Photographer: **Debbie Patterson**
Illustrator: **Lucinda Ganderton**

Typeset by MC Typeset Limited
Printed and bound in the United States

PICTURE CREDITS

Camera Press: page 132 bl (Rosemary Weller). The Garden
Picture Library: pages 24 b (Ron Sutherland); 57 b (Brigitte
Thomas); 83 r (Marijke Heuff); 136 (Steven Wooster); 137 tr
(Gary Rogers); 139 (Jane Legate). Robert Harding: page 144
b. Jerry Harpur: pages 12 b (designer: Patrick Presto, San
Francisco); 32 bl (designer: Keeyla Meadows, San
Francisco); 38 b (designer: Sonny Garcia, San Francisco);
101 t (designer: Thomas Church, San Francisco), bl
(designer: Cyrille Schiff, Los Angeles); 138 l (designer:
Sonny Garcia, San Francisco), r (designer: Vernon
Edenfield, Fredericksburg).

Contents

INTRODUCTION 6

PLANNING YOUR GARDEN ROOM 8

FLOORS AND FLOOR COVERINGS 20

WALLS AND WALL COVERINGS 34

SOFT FURNISHINGS 58

FIXTURES AND FURNITURE 78

ACCESSORIES AND DECORATIONS 104

LIVING IN THE GARDEN 128

PRACTICALITIES 148

Templates 152

Stockists and Suppliers 156

Index 158

Acknowledgements 160

Introduction

There is something very special and satisfying about having your own outdoor space, however small it may be. It is your own little patch of the world to pamper and enjoy without interference (you hope) from anyone else. It is a part of your home that just happens to be outside. And as a part of your home, there is no reason why you shouldn't decorate it in much the same way as you might go about decorating the rooms inside the house.

You can create impact by painting and staining fences, walls, furniture, and pots to complement the planting; you can use visual tricks to create perspective and romance; and you can finish it all off with outdoor pictures and decorations. These are just some of the hundreds of ideas in this book, which I hope will inspire you to think about your garden in a completely different way. You don't need special knowledge, and you don't have to spend hours toiling to keep it looking good. The aim is to create a delightful living space, craftily organized so that all the family has room to entertain, play, or simply relax there.

I do hope you find inspiration from the many pictures, suggestions, and step-by-step projects as you browse through these pages, so you can create an exquisite, personalized outdoor room of your own.

PLANNING YOUR GARDEN ROOM

Transform even the smallest plot
into an outdoor room by decorating and
furnishing it – in much the same way
as you might inside. With everything set out
to best effect, it will then be ready for you
to enjoy with family and friends at any time.

OPPOSITE: *A simple trellis arbor hung with*
lanterns, a wooden bench, a table and
candle light create a beautiful outdoor
room in which to enjoy summer evenings.

Major Considerations

The most comfortable and visually pleasing garden rooms are usually the result of careful planning. You will need to consider how best to use the available space, the vista, and the ambience before you prepare the "canvas" for the decorative touches. But once you begin to reap the rewards of such forethought, you will certainly feel it was all very worthwhile.

You will probably want somewhere to sit and, perhaps, eat. If you have children, you will want somewhere for them to play, and you will also need to allow for some kind of storage area for tools, pots, and other garden paraphernalia. All this is perfectly possible even in tiny gardens. An area 6½ ft square is sufficient space in which to sit and eat. Children would be thrilled with a sandpit just 3¼ ft square and, if there is just a little more space, there will be room enough for a small playhouse.

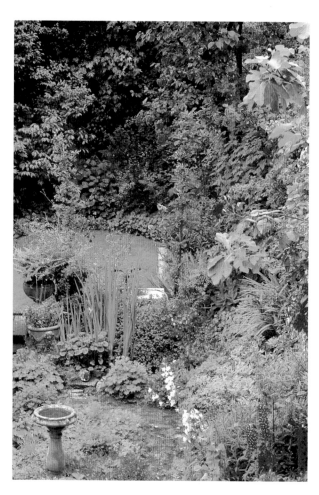

ABOVE: *Even light screening adds interest. Here, a line of neat iris leaves provides a boundary between the patio area and a delightful miniature lawn, lending importance to both.*

ABOVE: *By dividing up the spaces, you can create visual depth. These two huge box orbs help to define a vista and lend perspective to the arbor at the end.*

RIGHT: *Garden paraphernalia displayed on a delightful wire shelf transforms the functional into the decorative.*

ABOVE: *Low hedging is used here to form visual divides and create several rooms within one garden, for a rich and interesting design.*

Plan out in your mind the best place for each of these activities in much the same way as you might plan your kitchen, where you also need to provide space for working, eating, and leisure. Once these priorities are set, it will be much easier to work out the layout of the garden. This is important, even if you don't have the resources for new pavings and landscaping, at least for the foreseeable future. For example, there may be a flower bed just where you feel it would be best to create a seating area. With the garden layout left as it is, you would continually have to bring furniture in and out when you need it. That is no more comfortable than a sitting room would be if you had to bring in a chair every time you wanted to relax. However, with a few little changes, like simply turfing over the flower bed, you can organize the garden so it is ready for relaxation any time you want.

Once the main areas are worked out, it is much easier to decide where you want to have planting areas, and within this framework, you will be able to transform the space into a decorative outdoor room that you will want to use and enjoy for more than just the few summer months.

Planning for Privacy

You will only be able to relax in the garden once you have organized the basic needs: privacy and shelter. Without the benefit of enclosed spaces, especially in built-up areas, these considerations can be problematic. However, there are ways of achieving them. Trellis can be fixed on top of walls and fences to create extra height. You can then grow decorative climbers to provide a wonderful natural wallpaper. You could plant fast-growing conifers, such as thuja, though check their potential final height or you could end up deeply overshadowed, even if not overlooked.

Seating areas, in particular, need privacy. Even if you live in the middle of the country and have a huge garden, you will feel much more comfortable if you site these where, at least on one side, there is the protection of a wall of some sort. This could be the garden boundary wall, a hedge, or even a trellis screen to lend a more intimate feel. If you are closely overlooked, you may also want to create privacy from above. One of the most successful ways of doing this is to put up a pergola and let it become entwined with vines or other climbers. That way, you have a "roof," which filters the natural light and allows a free flow of fresh air.

ABOVE: *Hinting at secret spaces lends a romantic touch to any garden. This dividing wall hides part of the garden, offering privacy, while at the same time the archway framing a statue beyond gives perspective to the whole space.*

LEFT: *A Japanese maple, with stunning copper foliage, screens this seating area.*

RIGHT: *Secret places can be created in even the smallest of spaces. This pathway winds through plantings in a tiny 15-ft plot.*

Atmosphere and Romance

Once the space is defined, you can begin to set the mood. Creating ambience relies on stimulating the senses: sight, sound, touch, taste, and smell, all of which are supplied free of charge by nature. And simply by being outside, you are closer to nature, so it should be even easier to bring atmosphere and romance to the garden than anywhere else in your home. Stimulating each one of the senses is what this book is all about. The pages are packed with decorative ideas to enhance the garden.

These ideas can be set against the visual delights provided by the plants themselves. As well as the sound of the birds and buzzing insects, you can add the music of wind chimes or the evocative trickling of water in even the smallest plot. The outdoors also provides the most glorious fragrances, from sweet, from flowers such as roses, honeysuckle, and jasmine to aromatic, from lavender and piquant herbs. Touch, too, can be stimulated as it is impossible to walk through a garden without being touched by – or reaching out to touch – some of the plants, that is especially pleasing if they have interesting textures. Plan for a variety of these, including plants whose leaves range from fleshy to frondy and feathery. Finally, eating out in the garden contributes taste to complete the sensory picture.

The most romantic gardens hint at intimacy. They could literally be enclosed outdoor rooms, such as courtyards, balconies, or roof gardens, which automatically offer intimacy. If your space is large, you can add romantic interest by creating hidden places. This isn't difficult, even in the smallest garden. You can put a door in the fence or wall to hint at another space, put up an archway to give the feeling of moving from one area to another, or, perhaps, add a trellis screen to section off an eating area. As well as creating intimacy, these dividing tactics also create the illusion of space. Adding an archway or screen means you are able to see beyond into another area, which lends perspective to the whole space, giving it structure and shape. However light the resulting screening is, it hints at secret places and romance.

LEFT: *There is nothing more delicious than entertaining al fresco, when fresh seasonal food can be prepared without fuss and the table decorations are delightful in their simplicity.*

RIGHT: *The sound of trickling water enhances any outdoor area, and a water feature need not take up an inordinate amount of space. Water flows elegantly over this exquisite wall-mounted, cast-iron lily pad.*

BELOW: *A miniature courtyard is set out as an enchanting outdoor room. The cherry tree suggests pretty "wallpaper," while the blossom forms a natural carpet. Even a "coffee table" is positioned before the bench and an alcove is set in the wall.*

Finding the Levels

Whereas indoors, generally you would prefer your floor to be level, outside, the opposite is true. This is probably because inside, the various heights of furniture automatically give you interesting levels, and furniture tends to occupy a greater portion of floor space. Outside, even furnished·gardens offer greater expanses of floor space, which could result in monotony. Unless you have a very tiny space, the proportions of a room inside, or you have decided to have a very particular and probably formal design, such as a knot garden or parterre, you will probably want to create some changes in level.

Even a single step up from one area to another can do the trick. But if you are not in a position to completely relandscape for the sake of a few levels, there is still a lot you can do. You can add staging at one side, and use that to display potted plants. You can use a plant stand to lend a little height, and you can make a feature of garden buildings for higher-than-ground-level architectural interest. You can also use plants of various heights to create levels.

ABOVE: *Flowering climbers, such as clematis, don't have to be restricted to walls and fences. By training them up obelisks, you can take the color even higher.*

LEFT: *Even on a tiny patio area, there is room to create levels. Here, raised beds are built in white-painted brick to match the garden walls.*

OPPOSITE: *A pretty Victorian wire plant stand, filled with flowering plants, brings flashes of white high up in the middle of a largely green planting area.*

Planning the Planting

Herbaceous borders bring wonderful color in summer but die down to next to nothing in the winter, so it is good to provide an evergreen structure of plants to get you through all the seasons. These can also contribute to the "architecture" of the garden, creating levels, screens, and even sculpture. You can plan to have taller shrubs at the back of the borders, slowly graduating toward the front, or you can make more structured steps. You can arrange rows of small, lightly screening plants across the garden to create a living screen, and you can use specimen trees or neatly trimmed topiary as living sculpture.

The color scheme can be planned against this basic structure. The decorative garden room is at its prettiest with plenty of color. The structural shrubs and trees also can be chosen to make certain there is some color all the year round – fruit trees for blossom in spring; shrub roses for summer color; and late-flowering clematis and wonderful berries, such as those of the pyracantha, in autumn, and of holly in winter. This display can be complemented by autumn-flowering bulbs such as colchicum, schizostylis, and cyclamen.

But the most variety of colors can be added with pots and containers. There is always a choice of seasonal color at garden centers. By planting up in movable pots, you can put the color where you want it and replant with new seasonal color as the old blooms die. Pot up bulbs in the autumn for spring color and, as they die down, put them in a secluded part of the garden for their leaves to soak up the light, guaranteeing a better show next year.

Color creates much more impact if it is kept to a theme – of blues and pinks, perhaps, or oranges and yellows. This theme can be strengthened with the use of paint and stain on nearby fences, garden buildings, furniture, or even the pots themselves.

With the introduction of comfortable furniture, and with the finishing touches of accessories and decorations, a garden becomes an outdoor room ready for entertaining and relaxation.

BELOW: *You can use garden flowers outside in the same way as you might use potted plants inside. Here, spring flowers make a charming window display.*

ABOVE: *Conifers tied together at the top make a fabulous evergreen alternative to the classic rose arch.*

ABOVE: *A beautiful specimen plant, such as this rose, makes a delightful feature.*

RIGHT: *Seasonal flowers look lovely potted up and grouped for massed color. This also allows you to move the color around the garden whenever you want to.*

FLOORS AND FLOOR COVERINGS

The floor offers the basic structure to the
garden room, setting the tone in stone or brick,
gravel or grass. And even though these
elements may seem fixed, there is still scope for
decoration with imagination and flair.

OPPOSITE: *The flooring in this potager-
style plot is made up of a system of
pathways in brick paving that divides the
garden into distinct planting areas,
encompassing herbs, flowers, fruits,
and vegetables.*

The Place to Start

Outside, even more than in, the "floor" has a huge impact on the overall effect, and decorating your garden has to start with the groundwork. Perversely, the smaller the area, the harder the "floor" has to work. Where there is plenty of space, sweeping lawns are fine. Where space is at a premium, it may hardly seem worth getting the mower out, and a combination of hard and soft "flooring" becomes both more sensible and visually pleasing. Just as inside, the basic choice comes down to hard and soft flooring – the hard being patios and paths, the soft being planting. But while a single surface running seamlessly from wall to wall looks wonderful inside, outside, in anything but the smallest patio, it is likely to look flat and dull. Introduce variation, texture, and a change in levels to create a much more interesting vista.

If you can afford it, and you want to start from scratch, it really is worth getting the floor right, since that offers the best basic structure to the garden. Even the most charming planting, pots, and decorative details are diminished when set against uniform concrete slabs, while a well-thought-out floor looks elegant even

before the addition of a single plant. And, in later years, it will be much easier to completely change the planting, pots, even the boundaries in order to create a new look, than to restructure the ground.

Even if it really isn't feasible to go for major change, there are ways to improve the situation, perhaps by removing some of the slabs to increase the planting areas both around the perimeters and within the main paved areas. Or you could use decorative detailing to disguise parts of a less-than-pretty surface.

ABOVE: *Brick-shaped stone paving set into a tiny lawn, then decorated with miniature urns, mimics the vistas set out on the floors of classical gardens.*

LEFT: *The clay-tiled floor and brick retaining walls of an old greenhouse make an evocative home for a herb garden and a focal point within the whole context of this established garden. The same effect could be achieved using any vitrified tiles designed for pathways, laid diagonally in alternating colors.*

OPPOSITE: *This tapestry of purple and lilac bordering herringbone-laid brick is reminiscent of a soft carpet on parquet flooring. Mosses, alpines and other low-growing plants have been allowed to take up residence on the curved York stone steps.*

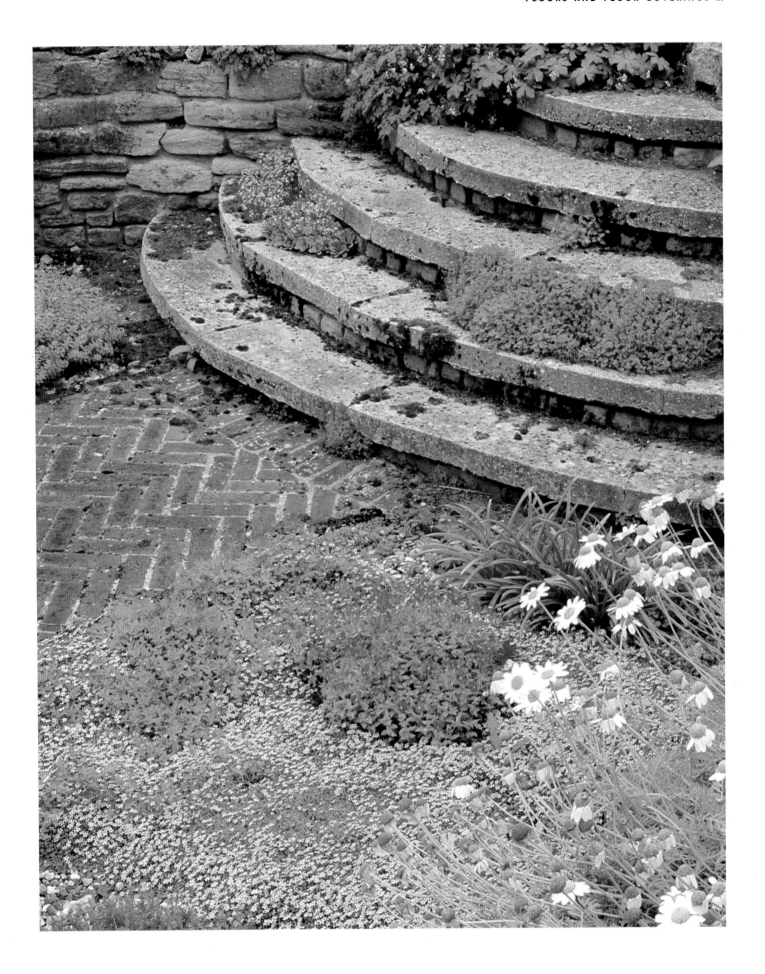

Material Choices

Outdoors, little surpasses the beauty of natural stone, especially if it is a local stone which inherently harmonizes with its surroundings. Another good material you can use is brick, which again, if it is a local brick, will naturally blend with the house and garden. Only bricks with a flat surface are suitable for outside use, and even then, some are not frostproof. It is best to choose brick paving, which is specially made for patios and paths. Aggregates are another kind of natural stone. These come in the form of gravel, which can be

LEFT: *Stone pavings, laid end to end, visually elongate the path in the garden of this town terrace.*

sharp but beds down well, or shingle, which has a similar appearance but, coming from the shore, has more rounded grains. Other decorative, naturally hard surfaces can be achieved with the clever use of pebbles, slate, or ceramics. The not-so-hard underfoot floorings come in wood, either as a custom-made timber decking or in the form of reclaimed materials, such as timbers from railroad tracks.

If natural hard flooring material is out of your price bracket, there is a wide choice of concrete paving. Not all come in uniform, uninspired slabs. Many have subtle variations in tone to give a naturally aged look and are available in varying sizes. Some come in the form of ready-to-split blocks of cobbles, each of which comes away slightly differently, giving a more natural, finished effect.

LEFT: *Timber decking makes a delightful alternative to stone or concrete for patios or outdoor living areas. It can also solve problems in gardens which slope by providing a level, raised platform from which to view the scene.*

When it comes to soft flooring, the most obvious solution is grass. Planting also offers a soft floor, though this is usually a look-but-don't-walk area.

The choice of material is one thing, deciding on its best form for your garden is quite another. Stone, natural or otherwise, is available in slabs, rectangles, small squares, cobbles, or crazy paving. Concrete also comes in any number of shapes, such as hexagons and octagons. The form you choose and the way in which the stones are laid can affect the whole look of the garden. Smaller units can make a tiny plot seem larger. Bricks laid widthwise across a path can make it seem calmer; laid lengthwise along the path, they lend dynamism. A herringbone arrangement is both attractive and lends a feeling of establishment, reminding us of the Elizabethan era. Using different-sized units of the same material offers variety, while diagonally laid rectangles can visually enlarge a tiny patio.

Changing the level in a garden immediately adds an extra dimension. Even a single step – perhaps up to a patio – gives the feeling of moving from one area to another, while lending visual depth to the whole gar-den. But beware, flights of more than two steps need plenty of space and can quickly eat into a small garden since each one needs to be at least 12 in deep. Flights of stairs leading down to the garden can be a real bonus because it doesn't take much effort to make a feature of them. Pots of plants on each step always look charm-ing, especially if they end in a flourish at the bottom with a carefully arranged group.

LEFT: *Miniature violas, one plant to a pot, make an enchanting decoration for old stone steps.*

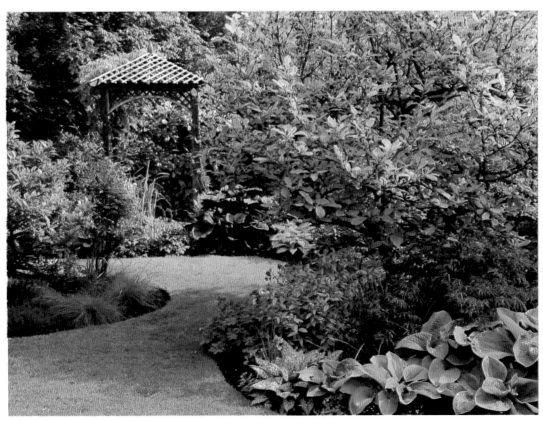

LEFT: *A sweeping lawn makes an enviable natural emerald carpet, perfect for damp climates.*

Floor Planting

Any kind of outdoor floor looks more established if small mosses, plants, and lichens are allowed to take up residence between the paved areas, though the finished effect can be greatly enhanced with a little judicious weeding. Self-seeded violas look enchanting; thistles aren't so appealing! On a slightly broader scale, you can cultivate mini-gardens or "lawns" by removing a paved area and planting instead. This is a particularly effective way of softening uninspired areas of large concrete slabs. Try planting a miniature herb lawn that releases its aroma as you brush past. Chamomile (the nonflowering variety "Treneague") and thyme are particularly effective. Or you can plant with larger herbs, such as lavender or sage. Low-growing flowers, such as alyssum, violets, violas, pinks, or any of the alpines, can offer a subtle but effective splash of floor-level color.

LEFT: *A carpet of tiny alpine strawberries gives this floor an appealing summer appearance.*

ABOVE: *This fascinating three-dimensional, ceramic sun makes an original floor feature. Planted up with low-growing plants, such as mind-your-own-business, it takes on the appearance of a rich green tapestry that enhances the sun motif.*

ABOVE: *This floor has been given an extra dimension with an alpine garden planted into an old millstone.*

Alpine Wheel

There is something very appealing about alpines. The wonderful variety and texture of the plants are punctuated in the spring with the most delicate-looking flowers. They are not difficult to look after, and will eventually spread to create a rich tapestry. This wheel makes a refreshing change from the more popular rock garden. Make it as small or as large as you like, and calculate the number of plants needed by checking their spread on the plant labels.

TOOLS AND MATERIALS

For a wheel about 8 ft in diameter:

2 × 6-in lengths of wood

String

Spade

Compost and fertilizer

Old drain cover

62 bricks

*About 3 alpine plants with a 12-in
  spread per section*

Gravel to cover

Pebbles and slates for decoration

1 *Make a simple pair of compasses using the two pieces of wood linked by a piece of string the length of the radius of the wheel. Dig over the approximate area of the wheel, and prepare the soil by adding compost and fertilizer. Using the compasses, mark out the circle, and place the drain cover in the center. Place bricks around the circle to form "spokes."*

2 *Position the plants as desired. In this wheel, each section has been planted with a different variety, so that as they grow they will help to define the design.*

3 *Sprinkle gravel between and around the plants, and finish the design with decorative pebbles and slates.*

Edgings

The way a path or a patio is edged plays an important part in the successful design of the flooring. Many of the well-designed concrete pavings and setts (small cobble-like pavings) have complementary kerb edgings. Another idea is to make edgings by laying paving in a different direction than the rest of the path or patio, or on their sides to provide a ridge; or to use bricks set at an angle to create a zigzag edge. There are also specially designed edgings in stone, brick, concrete, and metal. Also, you can create your own in, say, shells or by making a border of corks "planted" upright at the edge of a bed or you could create neat miniature hedging of box or lavender.

BELOW: *Scallop shells left over from the dinner table or cajoled from the fish store make a delightful edging in soft coral shades that coordinate well with terracotta pavings.*

LEFT: *Original Victorian rope edgings are enjoying renewed popularity, and many new ones are now available.*

RIGHT: *These antique, charcoal-colored, stone edgings would provide a neat finish to a town garden.*

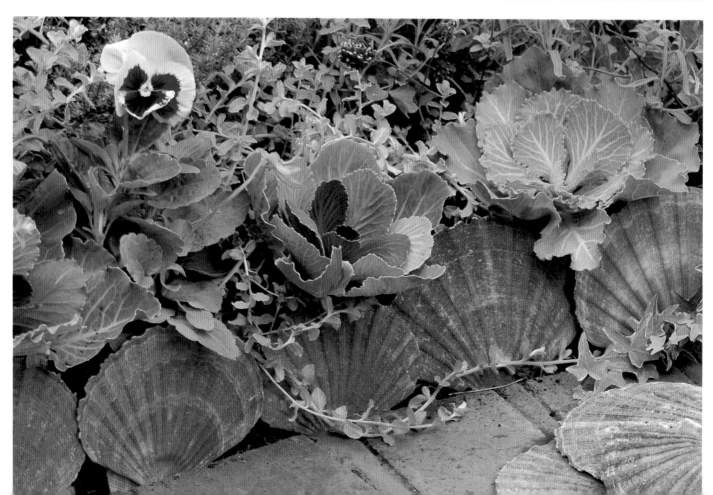

Making Patterns

There is a great tradition of elaborate "floors" for outside use. The Romans created intricate mosaics on courtyard floors, a skill that reached its zenith in richly decorated Islamic outdoor architecture. In the Middle East and India, decorative paths and walkways were composed of geometric patterns in ceramic tiles. Echoes of this style can be seen in Victorian English architecture where terraced houses have distinctive "tessellated" pathways, tiled in geometric patterns, usually forming squares, rectangles, and triangles in black and white or cream, chocolate and terracotta.

Pebbles are another mosaic material with a centuries'-old tradition. Their natural colors and smoothly rounded forms can be used to make exquisite textural panels or even complete garden floors. Again, simple geometric shapes are traditional, though in the hands of an artist given enough space, they can become elaborate, figurative works of art.

Floor patterns using plants have also been created through the ages. The most obvious examples of these are Elizabethan knot gardens and baroque parterres. An outline shape is formed using hedging in simple straight lines, geometric patterns, or curves to create, in the case of a knot garden, an elaborate knot effect. Traditionally, different plants are then planted within each section of the knot. Parterres can be on a much grander scale, often incorporating topiary, lawns, and highly formalized plantings.

ABOVE: *Tessellated tiles rescued from a crumbling public pathway, destined for a junk yard, make an enchanting detail in a flower border.*

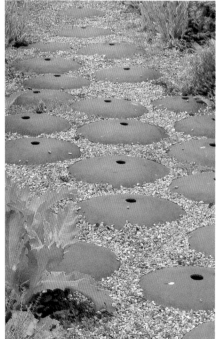

LEFT: *Even old hub caps from agricultural machinery can be used to add texture to an ordinary gravel pathway.*

LEFT: *A miniature parterre decorates the corner of a modern driveway.*

Pretty Pebble Rug

Create an outdoor "fireside rug" from pebbles, broken garden pots, and old china ginger-jar tops. The simple design is not difficult to achieve and makes an appealing, witty motif in a paved patio. However, a pebble panel like this will need to be laid at the same time as the rest of the paving. See the plan at the back of the book if you wish to follow this design in detail. This rug measures 2 × 3 ft and, although you could make one of any size, it would be easier to start off with a small one.

PREPARATION

First prepare the flat bed. If you are having your patio paved by contractors, you can ask them to do this, giving them the dimensions and position of the finished panel. The bed should be prepared to a depth of about 4 in, allowing a 2-in clearance below the level of the rest of the paving. If you are doing the paving yourself, dig a pit 6 in deep and to the dimensions of the panel. Mix equal parts of fine aggregate and cement. Then, using a watering can, dribble in a little water at a time until you have a dry, crumbly mix. Use this to fill the area, leaving a 2-in clearance. Allow the mix to dry. Gather together plenty of materials for the design and lay them out for size on the dry bed before you begin. Using tile cutters, cut off the bottoms of at least six terracotta pots and snip off the rims in sections. Choose pebbles and slates that are long enough to bed in at least 1 in below the surface of the "rug."

CARE

Protect the rug for three days by covering it with a board raised on bricks then overlaid by plastic sheeting. Avoid walking on the rug for a month to allow the mortar to set.

TOOLS AND MATERIALS

Spade
Fine aggregate to fill the area to a
   depth of 4 in
Cement
Watering can
Water for mixing
Selection of pebbles, pieces of slate,
   terracotta pots, china-pot lid tops
Tile cutters
Sharp sand
Mortar color
Straight edge
Hammer
Soft brush
Board to cover rug area
4 bricks
Plastic sheeting

1 *Prepare the mortar bedding by mixing equal quantities of sharp sand and cement. Add the mortar color. Mix in well. The design is worked while the mortar mix is dry, to enable you to change the design as you work. But the design has to be completed in a single day because moisture from the atmosphere will begin to set the mortar.*

2 *Pour the dry mix on to the flat bed and, using a straight edge, smooth it out until it is level with the rest of the paving. Then remove a small quantity from the center so the mix does not overflow as you work. This extracted mix can be readded at a later stage, if necessary, as the design of the pebble rug progresses.*

3 Starting from the outside and using the hammer, carefully tap in pebbles, slates, and the rim sections from the terracotta pots to make a level, decorative border.

4 Brush the mortar over the worked areas to make sure any gaps are filled. To build up the border design, continue working toward the center, carefully hammering in the pebbles, slates, and terracotta as you go. Use the china-pot lid tops to add a splash of color to the four corners.

5 Work out a central design using the terracotta bases, pebbles, and slate to provide a pleasing contrast with the border. Make sure the central area of mortar is flat. Then, using the tile cutters, cut the pieces of terracotta rim to size as necessary. Gently hammer everything into position. When the pattern is complete, brush the mortar evenly over the finished surface. Finally, using a watering can with a fine sprinkler nozzle, dampen the surface. As the mortar absorbs the moisture, it will set hard.

Decorative Details

It pays dividends to give attention to ground detail as well as everywhere else in the garden room, and that doesn't mean just the hard paving areas. Flower beds, too, can be treated to a little accessorizing!

Any collection of flat objects can be used to add interest. Pebbles collected from the beach, old pieces of tile, glazed ceramics, shells, or slates all look good when scattered on beds or in the tops of pots.

RIGHT: Even artifacts as unprepossessing as old drain covers can look good when grouped together on the floor, creating a pleasing effect with their natural geometry.

LEFT: Pieces of old slate, buried end-on into concrete, make a wonderful textural floor plaque. In spring, young forget-me-nots can be planted around it to create a vibrant azure border.

LEFT: Highly glazed frostproof tiles, bricks, and randomly shaped riven stone provide an unusual and decorative paving, reminiscent of a patchwork quilt.

Miniature Pebble Circle

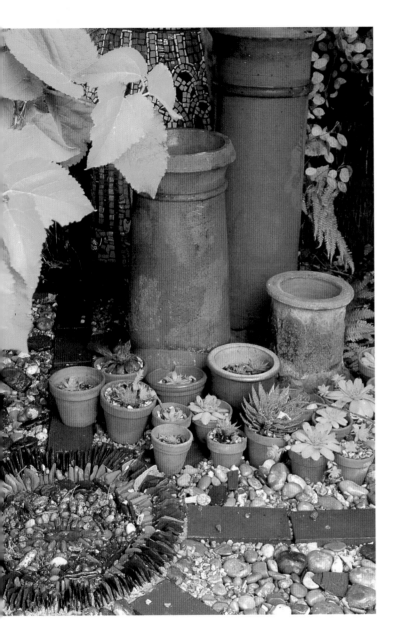

Here is a very simple mosaic made from pieces of slate and old terracotta plus a few beach pebbles, which can be used as a decorative detail anywhere in the garden.

TOOLS AND MATERIALS

11-lb bag of sand and cement mix
Mortar trowel
Slates, terracotta crocks, and pebbles

1 *Prepare a smooth circular area in the garden. Mark out the area for the finished circle using a makeshift pair of compasses (as described for the alpine wheel).*

2 *Add sufficient water to the sand-and-cement mix to achieve a crumbly consistency. Using a mortar trowel, smooth the cement into the circle.*

3 *Working quickly, before the cement sets, press in a border of slates.*

4 *Working in concentric rings, add a circle of old terracotta and another of slates, then a "wheel" of pebbles and terracotta.*

WALLS AND WALL COVERINGS

It is the garden walls – and the decorations
you put on them – that welcome visitors
at eye level. So dress the walls well, using
color, texture, pictures, and decorations.

OPPOSITE: *This ceramic tile panel makes
the ideal outdoor picture, perfectly
echoing its indoor cousin.*

Boundary Choices

Garden walls and fences are essentially functional. They are there to define the boundaries, to keep children and pets safely within and intruders out. Nevertheless, they also provide a design function, affording the garden its main vertical structure. Depending on the circumstances, this can be emphasized or played down. The obvious example for most houses is the contrast between the front and back gardens. In the front, fences are usually low or visually lightweight, creating a boundary without obscuring the house to provide an open, welcoming look. In the back, however, the boundary walls are more likely to be solid to provide privacy from neighboring gardens. They also form the background against which the garden can be planned. For this reason, the walls shouldn't be too dominant in themselves.

The most appealing garden walls have to be those of well-seasoned brick, evocative as they are of the walled gardens that are integral to large country homes. They lend an air of permanence, have a pleasing crumbly texture and, because they retain and reflect heat, they create a protected micro-climate within the garden. Garden walls always look best built with materials such

OPPOSITE: *Clambering creamy-yellow roses make a summer decoration for a flint-and-brick wall, taking over from a memorable spring flowering of wisteria.*

BELOW: *Picket fencing makes for a simple yet efficient boundary. Leave it regimentally plain or let climbers scramble over it, as here, for a softer look.*

as stone, flint, or stock brick. If you are building or repairing a wall, it is worth seeking out these traditional materials, even second-hand, as it will then blend in with its environment.

The most common garden "walls" consist of wooden lapped fencing, which is fortunately relatively inexpensive and easy to put up. It comes in panels, ready-treated against deterioration and is nailed to posts fixed into a "collar" of long metal spikes, which have been firmly driven into the ground. A similarly solid-looking wall is wattle fencing. Woven from young willow branches, this traditional fencing dates back to the Bronze Age in Britain. Still with its bark intact, it provides a fine texture against which plants can grow and clamber. Wattle fencing is available as "hurdles" (panels) of various widths and heights, which can be put up as quickly and easily as the more commonplace wooden fencing.

Plants, too, can be used to create garden walls. Box and privet offer classic hedging that is nevertheless very appealing, providing a rich green boundary all year around. It can also be clipped into simple topiary

ABOVE: *This living wall of roses makes a delightful garden boundary. Even grown over quite a flimsy frame of trelliswork or chain link, roses soon provide dense cover that protects privacy as much as any more solid planting.*

shapes, which look just as effective in small urban gardens as they do in larger rural ones. The trick is to keep them to the scale of the garden and its surroundings. Elaborate peacocks may look fantastic in the country, but in urban situations, a neat orb, or a stately obelisk would be more appropriate.

Larger conifers, such as thuja, can also provide lofty, verdant hedging, which is perfect for protecting your privacy in built-up areas. However, some conifers will eventually grow very tall – up to 50 ft – so make sure you buy one of the more manageable varieties, such as *Thuja* "Lutea Nana," which stops at a modest height of about 6 ft, or "Rheingold," which reaches 10–12 ft.

Another way of creating a living wall is to put up a trellis on which to grow climbers and ramblers. The classic choices are roses, honeysuckle, jasmine, clematis, and potato vine (*Solanum jasminoides*), all of which produce flowers, for a fabulous floral wall. Cleverly planted, they can provide color interest all year around. If your horticultural knowledge stops short of the encyclopedic, plan the easy way by buying a new climber in flower every two or three months. They will all come up again the following year, guaranteeing another lovely display of year-long color.

LEFT: *This decorative trellis features panelling at its base, which has been painted in the same way as for an interior. This yellow-green shade always looks attractive with plants.*

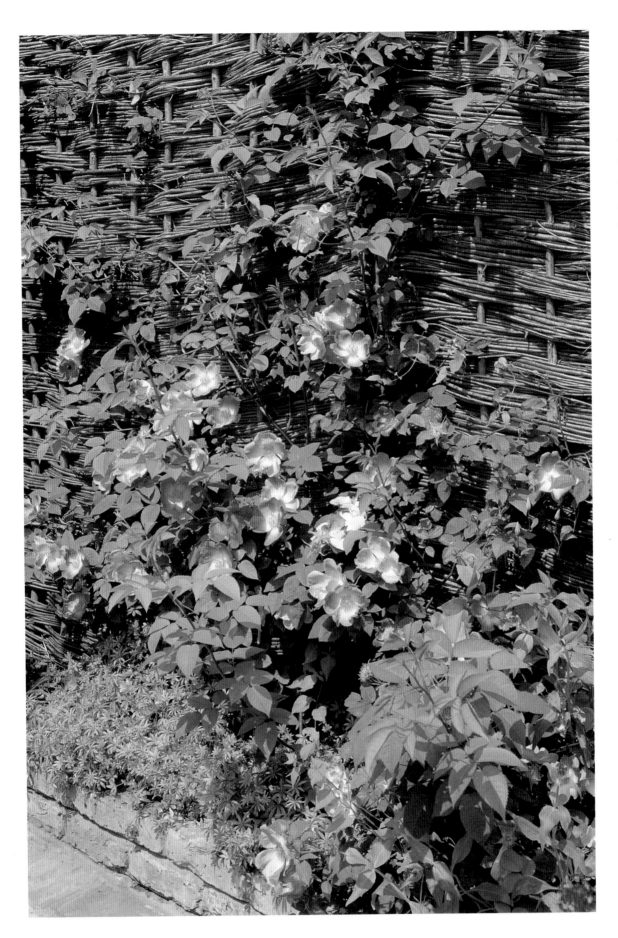

LEFT: *Wattle fencing has been used in Europe for centuries. Made of woven willow, it provides a wonderful texture to the garden and improves with age as plants grow up and through it.*

Fences and Dividers

Privacy is not always the priority. At the front of the house, you may prefer to be a little more open and welcoming, while still needing a fence to define the boundary. These lighter "screens" could be low walls teamed with low hedging, such as the traditional box or privet, or a pretty floral hedge, such as lavender or fuchsia. Wood can make decorative front fencing, too. Traditional picket fencing looks wonderful in classic,

LEFT: Metal railings are the classic smart answer for front gardens in town, but they are just as pleasing when used to divide a rambling country plot. The appeal is the smart, almost military line they make that unequivocably says "no entry" without obstructing the view.

clean white or it can be painted to complement the plants. In the country, rustic poles look good, especially if you don't want to obscure a wonderful view. They can be positioned either upright in lines or arranged in a series of long, low crosses to create a loose trellis. Metal is another perfect material for front fences. Railings, marching regimentally across the front garden, look smart in a city, while metal lattice or trellis work will look decorative in any situation.

Another setting for lightweight or low fences is within the garden, to divide off areas such as those where special plantings have been made or to define living areas or herb gardens.

LEFT: White-painted picket fencing provides a classic boundary marker that is perennially pleasing. The crisp, uniform line of wooden posts, with its picot edging at the top, provides a framework to the garden that looks smart anywhere.

ABOVE: *Crossed rustic poles bring charming restraint to unruly shrub roses.*

LEFT: *Metal trellis work, here decorated with charming cast-metal flowers, makes the most delightful front-garden fencing.*

Entrances and Exits

Depending on where they are, garden gates and doors have different functions and different decorative appeal. Front gates welcome visitors, directing them toward the front door, and so, like front fences, are generally lower and more screen-like in appearance. Gates and doors at the side of the garden and leading into the back serve quite the opposite purpose, that of protecting against intruders, so they are generally more solid. They also play a very different visual role in the general design of the garden. They offer a break in the possible monotony of the wall and, since their presence suggests they lead somewhere, they can also lend an intriguing extra dimension to the garden. Even if it doesn't actually go anywhere, a door in a wall or fence gives the romantic impression of leading to a secret garden or another, unknown space. It also allows us a feeling of privacy for we, too, are in a secret place, accessible only to those we allow in.

OPPOSITE: *An exquisite weathered wood and metal door makes a decorative garden entrance.*

ABOVE: *This tall, metal gate leads from one part of the garden to another, lending intrigue to a space that would have offered less interest had it been one large open area.*

ABOVE: *An ordinary, wooden-slat garden door leads from an alleyway to a tiny but enchanting city garden. The twig wreath gives just a hint of the delights to be found behind the door.*

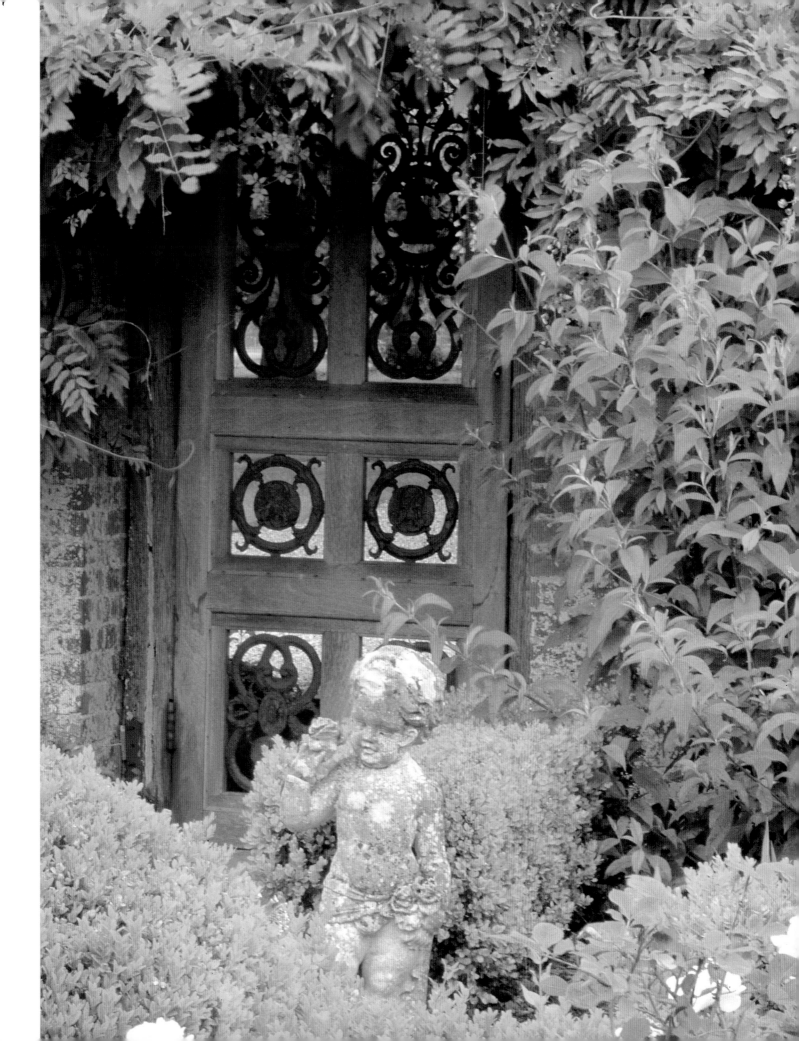

Trellis Work

Trellis is a great garden material. It can be used as a wall in itself, providing a framework for climbers and ramblers. It can be used as a divider within the garden to lend perspective (which is dealt with in more detail in *Fixtures and Furniture*). It can be used to give height to walls where extra privacy is needed, and it can be used to decorate the walls themselves. The decorative aspect is especially valuable where the walls or fences are less than beautiful or where you would like to add a little extra texture.

The trellis does not have to be ready-made. Old gates, an old window minus the panes, metal panels, or panels made from vines and other organic materials can all serve the same purpose as ordinary trellis work and have the advantage of looking good, even before the climbers have been planted. More traditional trellis work can also be given a head start with a touch of paint, which immediately provides it with a more finished and individual appearance.

ABOVE: *Here, painted square trellis has been used as a screen, dividing off one part of the garden. It provides an excellent framework for a climbing rose and clematis. This trellis can also be a pretty solution for a boundary wall.*

RIGHT: *An old wrought-iron gate provides an elegant trellis framework for a miniature rose.*

ABOVE: *A fabulous, Indian, metal trellis panel makes an imaginative framework for a special feature. The frame has been painted in verdigris colors, and duck-egg-blue urns planted with saxifrage complete the picture.*

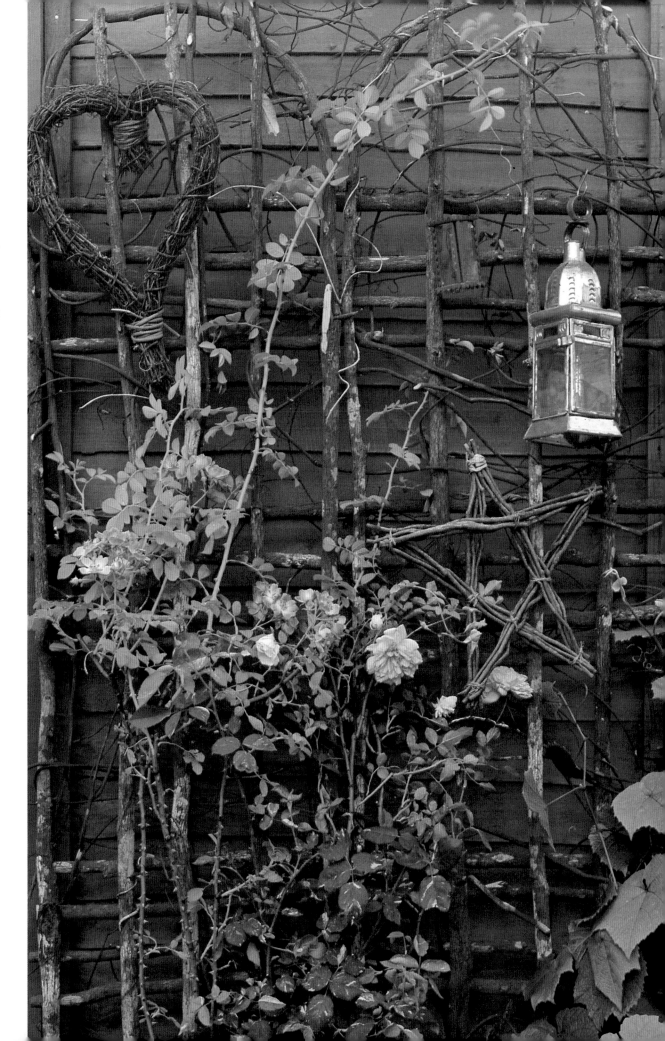

RIGHT: *Evocative, organic twig trellis panels make a wonderful framework for a montage of climbing roses and additional decorative features such as twiggy hearts and stars and metal lanterns.*

Adding Color

Inside the house, once the walls are plastered, you would immediately want to decorate them. Outside, people are still a little frightened of color, preferring to play safe by sticking to the natural tones of stone, brick, and wood. Nobody would dream of painting a beautiful old stone or brick wall, anyway. But if your new fencing is the popular panelled variety, it is likely to arrive coated in a preservative to protect it from deterioration, which usually comes in a violent shade of rust that you will probably want to cover up fast. In a decorative garden room, color is very important. Not only can the paint you choose suggest mood and ambience, just as it does inside, it can also be used to emphasize the color scheme of the planting.

The surfaces you paint may be the house walls, walls of outside buildings, or the garden walls. Maybe you have a hotchpotch of fencing and trellis work, all of slightly different woods and ages, that has resulted in a visual muddle. Paint them all in the same decorative finish, and you will have a much more coherent look. Or you may have newly erected trellis work that has a

ABOVE: *Sugared-almond shades differentiate the two properties. In the far garden, the pastel pink of the fencing perfectly matches the climbing rose behind.*

LEFT: *It is easy to create a strong impact by using the same shade on wall and furniture. Here, the trellis work and bench have been painted to match, creating a finished look even before the plants have become established.*

year or more to wait for a verdant covering of creepers. Paint it, and you will have a reasonable finish while you wait for the plants grow.

Color can also be used to highlight areas. You may pinpoint an area destined for a particular color scheme or you may wish to highlight the planting. Burnt-orange fencing would provide a stunning background for marigolds, while yellow picket would highlight the nodding heads of yellow pansies.

Painted fences and surfaces also lend color throughout the year. They are particularly valuable in winter

LEFT: *A decorative edge in stripes of bright Caribbean colors gives life to a plain white wall and door. Masking tape was used to keep the lines straight and, when they were all complete and dry, the leaves were stenciled in position.*

BELOW: *The texture of the brick work lends depth to any color you add.*

when many plants have died down. This is the ideal time to paint them with a fresh coat, bearing in mind the colors of the blooms that will come up in spring. It is not difficult to quickly add color as, unlike inside, you don't need a lot of time for preparation when the subject of your attention is rough-sawn wood. There is no need to fill holes or sand down the wood. Just give it a good scrub to clean it, and allow it to dry thoroughly before applying the color. If you plan to paint a house wall, however, you will obviously need to prepare the surface thoroughly, by removing dirt and loose paint with a stiff brush, before applying the color.

Ideas with Paint

Whether you want to paint your garden wall or a house wall that makes up part of the garden, there is plenty of inspiration to be had. Experiment not only with color but with technique. As well as straight color, you can create depth by layering the colors. Try *trompe l'oeil* effects such as marble, stone, slate, or moss. Stencil on to walls, use potato prints, choose geometric designs, or even add simple motifs. The trick is to consider the scale. These effects will have to be seen from much further away than they would be if used inside the house. Even a 30-ft garden is a good deal larger than the average room, so everything has to be exaggerated a little. Paint effects need to be a little less subtle; motifs, generally larger.

ABOVE: *A checkerboard pattern always makes a striking display and is a traditional design in many communities, so it is unlikely to date. This one in tan and terracotta was inspired by African decoration; the same design in china-blue and white would evoke Provence. A checkerboard is easy to paint. Like this one, it doesn't necessarily have to be neat and even. Little irregularities simply add to its charm. If you trust your eye, paint it freehand, using a fine brush to create the outline of each square and then filling it in later with a wider brush if the squares are large. If you prefer something more orderly, cut a large square stencil and position it on the wall. Checkerboard a whole wall if you are feeling adventurous or work it on window and door reveals and along baseboards.*

ABOVE: *This cascade of falling leaves was created using a potato print, which can be just as effective outside as inside. Choose a simple motif, like this oak leaf, and, using the point of a knife, gently "draw" the outline on to the cut surface of half of a large potato. Cut away the potato from around the outline to a depth of about ¼ in and "draw" in the veins. Give the wall a pale colorwash base. When that has fully dried, dip the potato into a darker shade of paint, stamp it on to a piece of newspaper to remove the excess, then stamp on to the wall.*

ABOVE: *Marbling makes the perfect effect for an outside wall, since it works best in oil-based paints that are ideal for outside use. It should be applied to a reasonably smooth surface. The veins are applied over a primer while it is still wet and further splashes of mineral spirits are added to soften the hard edges.*

ABOVE: *Evocative of the sunny Mediterranean, lemons and limes make wonderful motifs that anyone can manage. Use the template at the back of the book, if you wish. Paint the shapes randomly like this or make a* trompe l'oeil *by painting a simple shelf of plates decorated with lemons.*

ABOVE: *An unprepossessing garden or tool shed wall gives the impression of having the patina of time when stippled in shades of green and ocher to give a mossed effect. First apply a colorwash of a medium to dark green, then roll on a pale green, and, finally, stipple on some ocher.*

ABOVE: *Naive lizard-like animal motifs are traditional in many communities. This one, inspired by African art, is not dissimilar to motifs used by American Indians. Just one lizard in the corner of a sunny wall would transform it from the ordinary to something special. Use the template at the back of the book, if you wish.*

Decorating a Shed

Even the most unpromising garden buildings can be turned into something special. When this one was "inherited" with the garden, it was little more than a concrete block. With the addition of some plaster shapes and paint, it took on the appearance of a miniature Mediterranean villa.

TOOLS AND MATERIALS

Pencil

Cardboard

Scissors

MDF (medium-density
  fiberboard)

Jigsaw or fretsaw

Acrylic wood primer

Decorating brush

Dark-blue latex paint

Fine-textured masonry paint in
  white

Acrylic scumble glaze

Water for mixing

Artist's acrylic paint in light-blue,
  red, orange, and yellow

Soft cloths

Nails

Hammer

Stiff brush

Exterior tile adhesive

Selection of small, decorative
  plaster shapes from
    architectural plaster suppliers

Electrical tape

Panel pins

Natural sponge

Artist's brush

Polyurethane varnish

Decorating brush for varnish

2 *Paint both the door and the MDF shape with acrylic wood primer and allow to dry for one to two hours. Paint one coat of dark-blue latex paint, and allow to dry for two to three hours.*

3 *Mix up a glaze using fine-textured masonry paint, acrylic scumble glaze and a little water to the consistency of heavy cream, then tint with light-blue acrylic artist's color. Paint this on to the door and roof shape in the direction of the grain.*

1 *Draw a Moresque roof motif on the cardboard to fit the top of the door. Check the size against the door. Cut out, and place this template on the MDF, drawing around its shape. Cut out using a jigsaw or fretsaw.*

4 *Quickly wipe off the glaze with a soft cloth to knock back the color. Nail the MDF shape to the top of the door, and paint the nail heads with the pale-blue glaze.*

5 *Using a stiff brush, scrub the wall surfaces to remove the dirt. "Butter" exterior tile adhesive on to the surface of each decorative plaster shape. Attach them to the wall. Use electrical tape and panel pins to hold them while the adhesive dries overnight.*

6 *Remove the tape and pins, then paint the wall with one coat of fine-textured masonry paint, and allow to dry for four to six hours.*

7 *Tint three pots of acrylic scumble glaze with acrylic paint – one red, one orange, one yellow – to the consistency of light cream. Using a damp sponge, wipe the colors randomly on to the wall, blending the edges. Wipe off the excess with a cloth.*

8 *Using an artist's brush, stipple extra color into any detailing to add emphasis. Allow to dry for at least four hours. Once it is thoroughly dry, varnish the wall.*

Color-theme Plantings

Create impact in the garden by color-theming seasonal planting with the walls. This works best with plants in containers since the containers can be chosen or painted to tone with the walls, then planted with flowers in complementary colors. Once the blooms are over, they can be replaced by new plantings for the next season. You don't have to always match the colors. You may decide to use complementary or even contrasting colors, instead. In this way, the garden looks fresh and bright all year around, and you have several scene changes as the seasons pass.

BELOW: Fences stained in softer, bluish-gray greens set off all manner of greenery, including the foliage of this hebe. The pot has been painted in stripes to link the greens with the pink blooms.

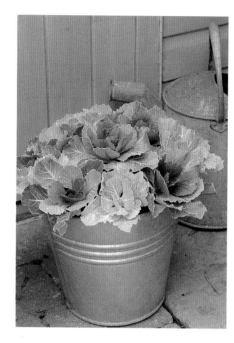

LEFT: The bluish-green and purple tones of ornamental cabbages look fabulous in an old galvanized bucket against the blue-green background of a painted fence.

ABOVE: *Blues and grays make a wonderful combination, and even the most rudimentary of garden paraphernalia can be put to good decorative use. This old, blue-painted wheelbarrow, set against a blue wall, creates impact, while making an original container for delicate blue violas.*

LEFT: *A yellow poppy and yellow violas look stunning planted up in golden pots, set against the warm ocher shades of a brick wall.*

Adding the Decorations

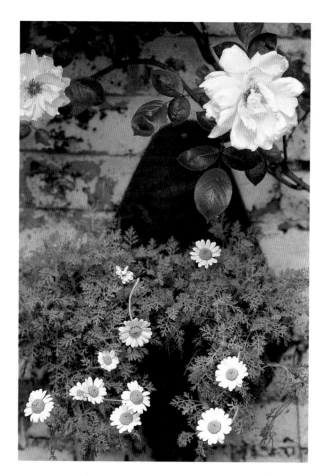

Once you are happy with the color of the walls, you can start to add a more personal touch with the decorations. The most obvious garden decorations are wall-hung pots, sconces, brackets, and small items of statuary. But almost any weatherproof collection could find a home on the garden wall. Bird cages, bird feeders, shells, lanterns, and willow or wire wreaths can be suspended on a wall. Or make a feature of wall-mounted shelves by filling them with pots, bottles, baskets, and enamel or galvanized ware.

LEFT: *A cast-iron wall sconce makes a charming container for miniature marguerites, peeping shyly through the more exuberant clambering golden roses.*

OPPOSITE: *This beautiful stone wall bracket makes the perfect garden "statuary" for a tiny patio.*

BELOW: *A group of galvanized containers makes a shapely collection on a cottage wall, their wonderful, soft metal shades blending harmoniously with the garden.*

Stone-effect Wall Mask

This wonderful stone-effect wall mask, evocative of medieval times, unbelievably started off as terracotta-colored plastic. The slightly pitted quality of the plastic makes it very suitable for painting, and once the mask is in position on the garden wall, surrounded by climbers, nobody will suspect that it is not made from natural stone.

TOOLS AND MATERIALS

Plastic wall mask

Medium-grade sandpaper

Acrylic primer

Decorating brush

Stone-colored latex paint

Acrylic scumble glaze

Artist's acrylic paint in raw umber, white, yellow ocher, and
*   burnt umber*

Water for thinning

Natural sponge

Large artist's brush

Matte Teflon-based polyurethane varnish

Decorating brush for varnish

1 *Sand the wall mask, and paint it with acrylic primer. Allow to dry for one to two hours. Paint with one coat of stone-colored latex paint. Allow to dry for two hours.*

2 *Tint some of the acrylic scumble glaze with a little raw umber, and thin with a little water. Sponge on to the mask. Allow to dry for one to two hours.*

3 *Tint some white acrylic paint with a little yellow ocher. Add to some scumble glaze and sponge on. Allow to dry for one to two hours.*

4 *Tint some more white acrylic paint with a little burnt umber, and thin with a little water. Load the artist's brush and spatter on to the mask in flicking movements. Allow to dry, and varnish.*

Pictures

Few walls inside the house are complete until the pictures are hung, and there is no reason why pictures should not be hung outside, too. They obviously need to be weatherproof, however, so the conventional indoor types would not be suitable. Ceramic tiled panels, mosaics, old enamel advertisements, or painted wood panels make excellent outdoor pictures.

RIGHT: *A quirky, ceramic, mosaic face sculpture smiles out through a "wall" of ivy.*

BELOW: *A pair of ceramic tile plaques echo the color of the painted arbors and furniture.*

SOFT FURNISHINGS

The garden's soft furnishings are its plants, so use them to special effect when decorating your outdoor room. Let them soften windows like curtains and create focal points of color like upholstery.

OPPOSITE: *Verdant greenery luxuriously drapes this window surround with a living curtain that echoes the most elaborate indoor window treatment.*

Decorative Plantings

Once the basic framework of the garden is in place, the fun can start with the soft furnishing. Inside, you would be thinking of comfortable furniture, curtains, and carpet. Outside, it is the planting that provides the soft furnishing. Without it, the garden would look very rigid and uninviting. Add a few plants and, immediately, it takes on a much more comfortable feel. This is the part of gardening that can be the most absorbing, even if you have no horticultural knowledge. A trip to a garden center to browse among the seasonal plants becomes a treat.

Putting together colors and textures to add to the border is where your own creativity comes in. But soft furnishing in our context is not just about borders. It is about all of the decorative planting that transforms an ordinary garden into a decorative garden room. It is about the climbers that clamber like curtains over arches and soften the outlines of windows, and the hanging baskets that decorate walls. It is about the low-growing plants that create carpets of color over what may previously have been uninspired floors. It is also about the plants that grow around and through old furniture in wilder gardens, creating a softness that hints at greater comfort. It is finally about the feature planting in containers, positioned at focal points of the garden to create added interest or greater impact.

ABOVE: *The face of a cherub, in reflective mood, peers through the ivy, adding a charming touch to the eaves of a garden shed.*

LEFT: *Statuesque Greek pithoi are used here for architectural interest, rather than for planting. However, they have been softened and beautifully set off by stately euphorbias in vibrant lime greens.*

OPPOSITE: *A floral arbor makes a rich decorative frame for a piece of statuary, creating a theatrical effect. The roses, foxgloves, and clematis make perfect stage curtains for this pensive stone player.*

Plants and Containers

The best way to create impact with seasonal flowers is to contain them in pots or some kind of container. This way, you can mass color in the plantings and group or stack the pots for an even greater show. Containers are fabulous in any garden – first, because the vessel itself, however simple, gives architectural form; second, because it allows you to put the plants and color exactly where you want them. You need a little color high up? Plant in a plant stand, hanging basket, or wall-mounted container. You need a little extra color in a flower bed? Add a colorful pot of flowering plants, setting it down among the greenery. You can even plant

ABOVE: *White violas in old terracotta pots, white-crusted with age, lend an ethereal air to the white-painted windowsill of the conservatory.*

in small pots to nestle on the top soil of larger ones for a rich, stacked effect.

Little matches the earthiness of ordinary clay pots. They blend happily with their surroundings and complement the plants. Make sure they are frostproof if they are outside when temperatures plummet, otherwise you will find the terracotta flaking off at the rim in the winter months.

Clay pots look different, depending on where they are from. Pots that are traditional in northern European countries, reminiscent of Beatrix Potter stories, are generally very red in hue, but the color does soften with age as salts naturally form on the surface. You can hasten this look by scrubbing them with garden lime. Just make up a thick paste by adding a little water to

LEFT: *Ornate Chinese ceramic pots make a delightful decorative feature when planted with toning flowering plants such as geraniums and petunias, and accessorized with complementary Chinese statues.*

ABOVE: *For a gloriously rich, banked window display, one window box has been placed on the front edge of the windowsill, while the other sits on the ledge. The planting scheme of petunias and dianthus in pinks and purples creates a greater impact for being color coordinated and is complemented by the glorious lilac orbs of the alliums in the foreground.*

the lime, then brush it on with an old scrub brush. As the water in the lime dries out, the terracotta will acquire a soft, white bloom. Garden lime is excellent since it is not harmful to the garden. In fact, it is used as a fertilizer, and it won't inhibit the natural mold growth that also, with time, enhances the patina. Pots can also be aged by rubbing them with natural yogurt, then leaving them in a damp, shady place to encourage mold growth.

Clay pots from the Mediterranean look very different than those of northern Europe. For example, Greek pithoi, traditionally used to store grain and oil, come in many elegant shapes and have a wonderful sandy color. Some are even frostproof.

Your choice does not have to be restricted to garden pots. Any container will do, as long as drainage holes can be drilled in the base. Try using old beer-barrel halves, decorative ceramic pots (many are now being imported from the Far East), old chimney pots, buckets, apple baskets, or traditional garden baskets, such as wooden trugs. With a little imagination, shopping baskets, bird cages, and lanterns can become hanging baskets; or decorative olive-oil cans in a row can become window boxes.

ABOVE: *All kinds of things can be used to add height to planting — particularly useful in spring and early summer when plants are still low. Here, a metal, stacking pan storage tower makes for brilliant high-level planting.*

ABOVE: *Even a couple of ordinary terracotta garden pots, hanging on the wall make an interesting decorative detail, especially when they are both planted with a froth of white blooms.*

Decorating and Planting a Window Box

Window boxes provide a delightful finish to windows, almost bringing the garden into the house. Being flat-fronted, they are also easier to decorate than rounded pots. Here, mussel shells lend impact to a coordinated planting of lavender and violas. Experiment with different shapes, using some mussel shells face up and others face down.

TOOLS AND MATERIALS

Small terracotta window box

Mussel shells

Glue gun and hot-wax glue sticks

Crocks or pebbles

Compost

Trowel

Water-retaining granules

Fertilizer granules

2 lavender plants

Tray of young viola plants

Watering can

1 *When you are satisfied with your design, glue the shells on to the window box, using a glue gun and hot-wax glue sticks.*

2 *Place crocks or pebbles over the drainage holes inside the window box.*

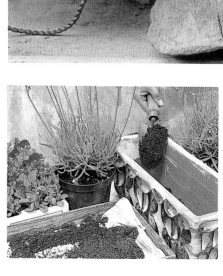

3 *Partly fill the box with compost, adding water-retaining and fertilizer granules as you go.*

4 Place the lavender at the back of the box. Press extra compost in front of them until it is the right height for the violas. Plant the violas on this "raised bed."

5 Press more compost firmly around all the plants, and water generously.

Hanging Gardens

When you want color high up or relating to the building, the easiest way is to create a hanging garden, either in a basket or in a wall-mounted container. Ready-made hanging baskets are designed so that as the flowers grow, they cascade through the side struts and spill over the edge in a joyous show of color, soon covering the whole basket. An alternative is to make the basket or container part of the display. Ordinary shopping baskets, buckets, agricultural containers, even kitchen equipment, such as colanders, pots, and pans, can all be used as hanging baskets.

If the containers are large and possibly too heavy to be supported, one trick is to put a layer of broken up expanded polystyrene (from plant trays or electrical goods packaging) in the bottom of the container. This is lighter than the equivalent amount of compost and provides good drainage. Containers should have drainage holes, and baskets will need lining to stop the soil from being washed out while you are watering. Liners can be homemade from a piece of plastic cut to size, with a layer of moss tucked between the basket and plastic for a more decorative look. As an alternative, you can use a proprietary liner, made from paper pulp, to fit purpose-made hanging baskets, or coconut matting which comes in a variety of shapes and sizes to adapt to all kinds of baskets.

Whatever type of container you choose, it needs to be filled with a good compost, and adding fertilizer granules and water-retaining granules can also help promote luscious results.

ABOVE: *The most unlikely items can be used as hanging baskets. This pretty metal lantern from the Middle East has been filled with terracotta pots planted with variegated ivies, to make a surprising and decorative hanging feature.*

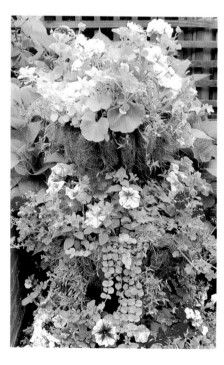

ABOVE: *Wall-mounted, miniature mangers stacked one over the other make a vibrant column of color in a tiny courtyard garden.*

ABOVE: *A witty interpretation of a hanging basket, this Indian bird cage makes an ideal receptacle for potted plants. Hung in a mulberry tree, it lends floral interest in early spring before the leaves have burst.*

Planting a Summer Basket

Hanging baskets are summer favorites in even the smallest of gardens, bringing a floral splash and fragrance, if you choose appropriate plants, to walls, verandas, patios, and even basement areas. Plant them early in the year, once the threat of late frosts has passed, to give them time to "get their toes in" and fill out.

TOOLS AND MATERIALS

Hanging basket with chains or rope

Coconut liner

Compost

Trowel

Water-retaining granules

Fertilizer granules

6 variegated ivies

Bucket of water

2 diascia

6 verbenas

Watering can

1 *Line the basket with coconut liner and partly fill with compost, adding water-retaining granules and fertilizer granules as you go.*

2 *Separate the ivy plants. Then thread them through the sides of the basket. Place a diascia plant at both ends of the basket. Add the verbenas.*

3 *Press more compost around each plant and down the sides of the basket so that they are all firmly bedded in. Water generously, and hang the basket.*

Color-splash Plantings

Just as you can decorate the inside of the home with colorful flower arrangements, so you can outside. Use pots of flowering plants to provide a colorful splash in a prominent part of the garden or to decorate the outdoor living area when entertaining. Create an immediate color impact by choosing a color theme and teaming containers and plants in toning shades. Try painting some terracotta pots to match your favorite flowers. You could also make a tablescape for a special occasion, using a variety of containers and seasonal flowering plants in perhaps hot, clashing colors or in cool shades of blue, purple, and white.

ABOVE: *Create a color splash for summer parties. Here, hot colors vie and clash in a fabulous, vibrant display. Simple enamel tableware and a wire "coffee pot" make witty containers for strawberry plants, geraniums, verbenas in magenta and scarlet, pansies, and daisy-like, yellow creeping zinnia.*

ABOVE: *White-painted terracotta pots planted with lily of the valley and placed on a stone bracket, make a supremely elegant feature during the spring.*

ABOVE RIGHT: *A selection of auriculas planted in an old stone urn and overhung with berberis makes a rich spring planting in shades of burnished copper, reminiscent of an old sepia photograph.*

RIGHT: *The bluish-green leaves of the pinks and oxalis perfectly complement the rich verdigris patina on this old, copper builder's bucket from France, creating a striking feature that can be hung in the garden or near the house. It's a brilliant way to bring color up to eye level in spring, when the plants are still low.*

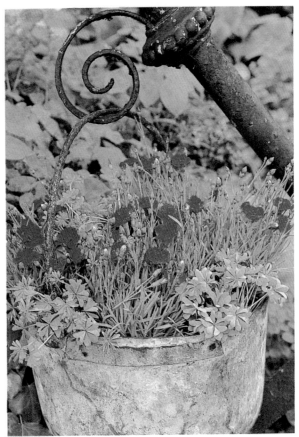

Creating Cameo Gardens

It is delightful to plan cameo gardens within gardens. They can provide a surprise in a small corner, enhance a less-than-full area, or even provide a miniature project for children who would love to have an area of their own. The idea is to find a theme – herbs, pansies, miniature vegetables, or lavender, for instance – then make up a "sampler," using a different container for each variety. As an alternative, you can make the containers the theme, choosing watering cans, culinary pots, pans and colanders, enamelware or terracotta in different shapes and sizes. Another idea is to design a miniature formal garden, perhaps taking inspiration from the classic Italian style. Choose a piece of miniature statuary as a focal point, then clip some young box plants into a miniature hedge around it, and fill in with a dwarf lavender.

LEFT: *An old lead sink becomes home to a decorative miniature vegetable garden. Two varieties of lettuce and one of mint – restrained from over-exuberant growth by being planted within its own concealed pot – provide a pleasing textural variety.*

LEFT: *Thyme gardens have a history that goes back through the centuries. Their appeal is the irresistible aroma combined with the almost endless number of varieties, with leaves that range in shape from round to needle-like; in texture, from smooth to woolly; in color, from silver to darkest green. The trick is to choose a selection to create a rich tapestry. Planting them in small terracotta pots keeps the garden to a scale in which the miniature size of the leaves and their various textures can be appreciated.*

RIGHT: *This terracotta garden is focused around tall flowerpots planted with hostas, ivies, and clematis left loose so that it behaves like a trailer, rather than a climber. Old drain covers and edging tiles add richness.*

BELOW: *Serried ranks of watering cans in the soft grays of weathered, galvanized metal make a beautiful feature in themselves. Planted with hostas and violas, they become a highly original cameo garden.*

Tin-can Plant Nursery

Seedlings can be decorative in themselves, so prick them out from their seed trays into a collection of aluminum cans mounted on to a plaque. They can grow there, high above any threatening late frosts, until they are ready to be planted out. The plaque itself looks wonderful made from ordinary aluminum cans, but if you want to add a bit more color, scour gourmet shops, and enjoy some culinary treats at the same time.

TOOLS AND MATERIALS

Piece of plywood, about 24 × 12 in

Primer

Colored glossy paint

Decorating brush

Can opener

Variety of empty aluminum cans with the labels removed

Metal cutters

Pliers

Nail

Hammer

Box of carpet tacks

1 Apply a primer followed by a coat of glossy paint to the plywood, allowing each coat to dry completely.

2 Use the can opener to remove the top of each can if this has not already been done. Wash out the cans thoroughly.

3 Using metal cutters, cut down the side of each can and cut off half of the base.

4 Open out the sides with pliers and cut a V-shape into each one. Pierce the base of each can, using a nail and hammer.

5 Try out the arrangement of the cans on the painted board. Then, using one carpet tack at each side point of the cans, nail into position.

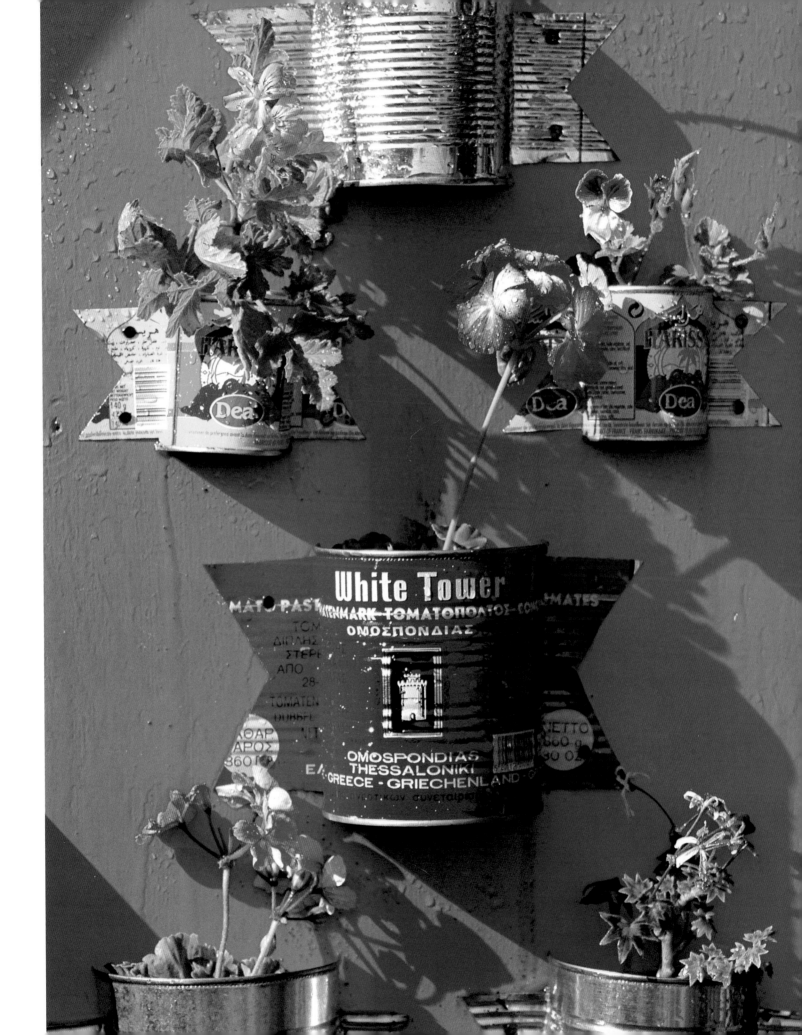

Whimsical Ways with Plants

Interesting gardens don't have to depend on a horticulturalist's knowledge of plants. Even the most ordinary plants can take on an exotic personality if pruned or planted in an original way. Many garden centers now sell ready-trained or standardized shrubs. Add your own touch with a decorated container, pretty underplanting, or an attractive way of tying them up.

Topiary has come back into fashion, but this time it isn't restricted to large, formal gardens tended by teams of gardeners. Box and privet grown in pots can be kept to a manageable size and still be clipped into architectural globes and conical shapes.

LEFT: *As a change from allowing roses to scramble up walls or trellises, this one has been trained around a simple obelisk, the diagonally trailing stems adding greatly to its decorative appeal.*

LEFT: *Small-scale topiary can be arranged, as here, in groups or used as boundary markers, down the edges of paths, between beds, or to section off different parts of the garden.*

LEFT: *A standardized hydrangea grown in a pot makes an excellent patio plant. It has the appealing appearance of a miniature tree, and you can enjoy its flamboyant blooms without any worry that it might take over the garden.*

FIXTURES
AND
FURNITURE

Fixtures such as sheds, arches, screens,
and shelving are the elements that begin to
give structure to the garden. Add a few
well-chosen items of furniture, and
the outdoor living is easy.

OPPOSITE: *A gracious walkway of fruit
trees trained over arches leads to a water
feature bordered by orbs of clipped box.*

Dividers and Arches

Even the smallest garden can accommodate fixtures such as arches, arbors, pergolas, trellis divides, or a small garden shed or playhouse. And while the hard landscaping and the herbaceous borders dictate the layout of the garden, it is these vertical elements that greatly affect its structure and overall look. Vertical structures such as pergolas and garden buildings can be positioned around the garden's perimeter, while rose arches, walkways, and trellis screens can be used as dividers. Anything that divides the garden lends extra perspective because it defines another space and, even in gardens that are fairly limited in size, being able to glimpse beyond into another area creates the illusion of greater space.

If you want to screen off part of the garden to create an eating area, perhaps, or to section off a vegetable garden, the simplest solution is to use trellis. Trellis is wonderfully versatile and comes in a variety of panel shapes and sizes. As well as the basic rectangular panels, there are panels with pointed, convex, or concave tops and even with integral "windows," all of which provide plenty of scope for creativity. When it comes to finishing touches, there is a wide choice of attractive finials in shapes such as globes, acorns, pineapples, and obelisks.

You don't have to screen off a whole area to lend perspective. Even a rose arch spanning the garden path can have the desired effect. Either buy a ready-made metal arch or make a simple wooden one using pergola poles or posts with short rafters or crossbeams across the top. Another way of making an arch is to use the plants themselves, planting young trees on both sides of a path, for example, then tying them together at the top so they grow into an arch.

ABOVE: *Trellis screens can divide off part of the garden to create the illusion of space or to emphasize a focal point – in this case, a water feature. Trellis panels come in a wide variety of sizes and shapes, and the supporting posts can be finished off with architectural finials such as globes or obelisks. The screen can then be painted for a decorative finish.*

ABOVE: *Here, a couple of young firs have been trained on to a metal frame to create what will eventually grow into a surprisingly substantial archway over this gravel path.*

LEFT: *Roses scrambling over an archway are a quintessential ingredient of a country garden. As well as bringing a delightful froth of blooms high above their natural position, the archway creates a simple screening effect that offers an illusion of space.*

Walkways, Pergolas, and Arbors

As well as serving as a light screen, arches can mark the beginning of a walkway. If you have sufficient space in the garden, a walkway has great appeal. There is something peaceful and cloister-like about a walkway beneath a leafy tunnel through which natural light filters to the ground. Even in a small garden, a simple, verdant archway offers a sense of romantic adventure, as if going to an enchanted place.

Walkways can be as simple as an elongated archway – probably the best option in small gardens – or a long snaking affair down one side of the garden. They can be made from metal or from wooden poles in a series of archways. The effect of a walkway can be made even more powerful if punctuated at the end by a focal point, classical style. In a formal garden, this may all have been planned as part of the landscaping, the walkway leading, perhaps, to a door or gateway, or an exquisite piece of garden statuary. But you can adapt the idea for a more modest setting and create impact. A specimen plant or a favorite pot, or a container with beautiful plants will provide a satisfying focal point at the end of the walkway, while acquiring a greater sense of importance for itself as it attracts the attention of everyone who saunters there.

Pergolas are first cousins to walkways, being covered areas usually placed on one side of the house. These work well in all sizes of gardens, providing an attractive, natural, covered outdoor "room" and serving as a transition area between the inside and outside. They make delightful, shady outdoor eating areas that afford extra privacy from overlooking apartments or close neighbors in buildings with terraces.

Leafy arbors can lend architectural form to a garden while taking up very little space. Tucked against a wall, an arbor can create structure in even the smallest garden, offering somewhere shady to sit, relax, and perhaps read or chat with a friend. At its simplest, an arbor could be formed by training climbing plants up a wall to form an arch over a garden bench, though it is not difficult to make a more permanent structure.

LEFT: *Flanked by greenery and shaded overhead by a roof of honeysuckle, this delightful arbor is set against the fabulous texture of a brick-and-flint wall. By incorporating the existing structure of the garden, it takes on an authentic "lived-in" feel. The weathered, rustic wooden bench and table are left out throughout the year, offering further structure to that part of the garden.*

ABOVE: *Cascades of laburnum make a flamboyant golden walkway.*

ABOVE: *This pagoda-topped metal walkway lends an almost oriental feel to the garden. Beautiful old Greek pithoi set in a bed of vibrant euphorbia and hellebores are used to great effect as the focal point at the end.*

RIGHT: *A simple timber framework forms the "bones" of this pergola, but once the climbers have grown over the structure, it is transformed into a lavish outdoor living area, decorated with a natural verdant wall covering.*

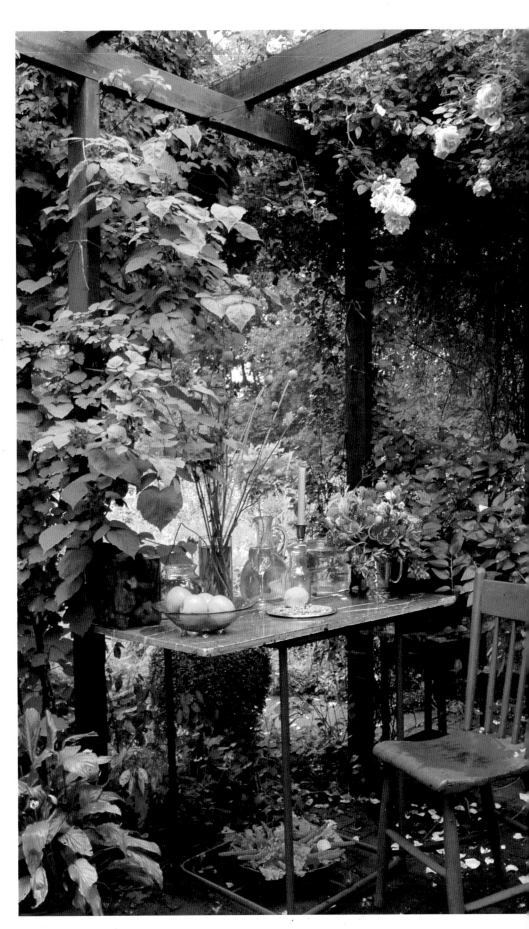

Trellis Arbor

An arbor is one of the easiest ways to introduce architectural structure to even the smallest of gardens, and it is no more difficult to make one than it is to put up a fence. This arbor is made up of trellis panels, then painted with a decorative outdoor stain to blend with the bench. The result is an enchanting, original bower.

TOOLS AND MATERIALS

Lattice (diagonal) trellis in the
following panels:
3 panels 6 × 2 ft
2 panels 6 × 1 ft
1 concave panel 6 × 1½ ft
1 panel 6 × 3 ft
6 timber posts 3 × 3 in, each 7 ft
long
Saw
6 spiked metal post supports
3 × 3 in, each 2½ ft long
Mallet
10 × 2-in galvanized nails
Hammer
Electric drill with No.8 bit, and
screwdriver attachment
40 × 1¼-in No.10 zinc-coated
steel screws
½ gallon can exterior
woodstain
Small decorating brush

1 Gather together the trellis panels and "dry assemble" to be certain you are happy with the design. Two of the 6 × 2-ft panels are for the sides and the third is for the top. The two narrow panels and the concave panel are for the front and the 6 × 3-ft panel is to be used horizontally at the top of the back. Trim the wooden posts to length. They should be 6 ft plus the depth of the metal "shoe" at the top of the metal spike which will hold the post.

2 Start with the back panel. The posts need to be placed 6 ft apart. Mark their positions. Then, using a mallet, drive in a spiked metal post. Drive a ready-trimmed post into each of the metal "shoes." Using the galvanized nails and the hammer, temporarily attach the top of the trellis to the top of the posts. Using a No.8 bit, drill holes for the screws at intervals down each side of the trellis. Screw in the screws.

3 In the same way, position the front outside posts and attach the side panels, then the inside front posts and front panels. Attach the concave panel to the panels on both sides of it. Finally, attach the roof in position, screwing it into the posts. Paint the arbor with exterior decorative woodstain and leave to dry.

Garden Buildings

Any kind of garden building adds to the outdoor architecture, and there are few gardens that don't have one, be it a garden shed, summerhouse, playhouse, or a gazebo. They are usually left just as they were when they were put up, but it is never too late to turn them into decorative features in their own right. Garden sheds can be decorated, for example, in stripes, like a cabana, or given a more substantial-looking roof of slates. Climbers can be grown up them or pots grouped around them. Playhouses, too, can be decorated to give them fairy-tale appeal. Honeysuckle or clematis could be grown over the roof, and hanging baskets hung under the eaves.

Purely decorative buildings were favorites in Victorian gardens as were ornamental Japanese or oriental gardens. It is easy to incorporate some fun in the form of a Gothic shed, pagoda, or temple. These can be bought ready to put up, or you could scour architectural salvage yards for doors and windows that can be assembled into a new design.

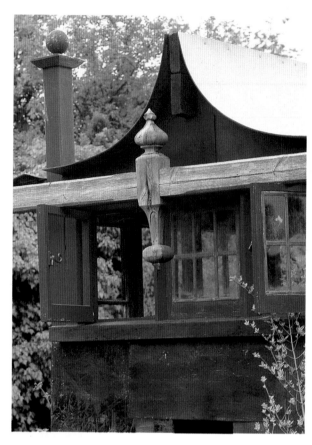

ABOVE: *Architectural salvage, some pillars and posts, plus a touch of paint make an eye-catching, latter-day garden feature.*

LEFT: *A traditional gazebo, complete with pagoda roof, makes a charming outdoor seating area while adding architectural interest to a small garden.*

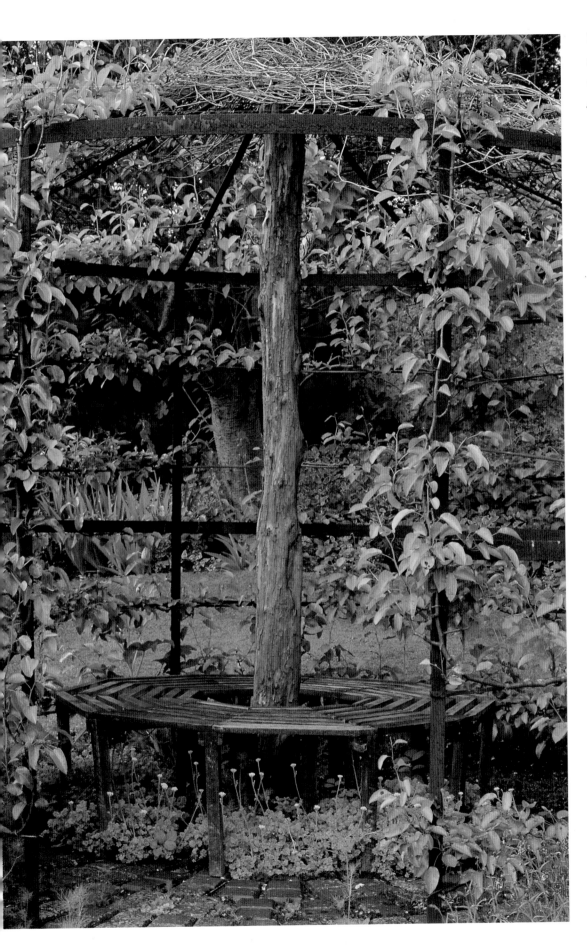

LEFT: *This delightful gazebo is simply made from a metal frame overgrown with climbers.*

Customized Playhouse

You can create an enchanting fairy-tale house that will add interest to the garden while providing a play area the children will love. Give yourself a head start by buying one off the shelf and customizing it. Playhouses usually come pretreated against decay which means they already have an excellent base for decoration, but do check this before you buy. This one has been given a slate roof with terracotta baby ridge tiles, shutters, and a decorative fascia and, finally, a coat or two of paint. This represents quite a few skills, so you could restrict yourself simply to painting the playhouse.

TOOLS AND MATERIALS

Playhouse

Roof slates – enough to cover the roof plus half as much again and one extra row of slates

Craft knife

Metal straight edge

2 × ¾-in nails per slate

Hammer

2 pairs of louvered shutters to fit the windows (choose a larger size if the exact size is not available)

Hacksaw

Electric drill with screwdriver attachment

8 nonferrous hinges

4 door magnets

Oil-based paint

2-in decorating brush

Polyurethane varnish

Baby ridge tiles to cover the length of the ridge

Premixed sand and cement

Cement board

Trowel

Decorative fascia precut from MDF (medium-density fiber-board) or a strip of MDF and a jigsaw to cut your own fascia (see template at back of book)

Saw

16 × 12-in paper for pattern making

ATTACHING THE ROOF SLATES

Work out how many slates you need for each row. If the slates don't fit the exact width, place as many whole slates in the bottom row as it will take, then cut two equal strips of slate to fill in at each end. Score and snap each slate in half widthwise. Place in position by hammering the nails through the predrilled holes and roofing felt. The next row of slates will completely cover the first row of half slates. Arrange them so the side edge of each slate runs down the center of the slate below it. Place in position as before. Position the third row so that the slates lie across the width in the same way as the first row. The bottom of the third row should line up with the top of the first row of half slates. Lay the fourth row like the second row, and so on.

ATTACHING THE SHUTTERS

Remove the windowpane divides. If the shutters are larger than the window opening, cut the opening to fit using a hacksaw. Attach the shutters using hinges, reuse the window divides as shutter stops and attach the door magnets.

DECORATING

Paint the playhouse with oil-based paint, and allow to dry for four hours in fine weather. Then finish with a coat of polyurethane varnish.

ADDING THE RIDGE TILES

Mix the sand and cement according to the manufacturer's instructions. Fill each end of each ridge tile with the mixture and "butter" some along the length. Bed into position.

ADDING THE FASCIA

Cut the fascia to length with the saw. Make a paper pattern of the top point of the roof, and use it to cut the fascia ends to this angle. Paint the fascia and place in position by predrilling pilot holes, then nailing it to the front edge of the playhouse roof.

ABOVE: *The original playhouse had a simple wood finish, treated against decay.*

ABOVE: *The roof slates and shutters are in position, and the playhouse has been decorated with an oil-based paint.*

ABOVE: *The original window divides have been reused as shutter stops, and door magnets have been positioned to hold the shutters closed.*

Water Features

Of all garden fixtures, water features must be the most entrancing. The gentle sound of water trickling, pattering, or gurgling has a wonderfully relaxing effect and the glinting, reflective surface brings a new dimension to the garden. It doesn't have to be a grand affair. There is room for a water feature in even the smallest backyard. At its simplest, it could be just a pipe, gently splashing water on to a pile of pebbles below. Water features can range from a miniature fountain bubbling

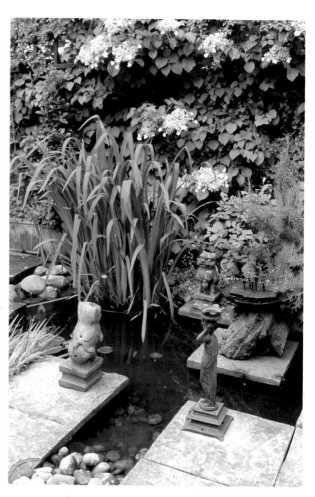

ABOVE: *A formal geometric pond with oriental overtones makes a charming focal point in a terraced town garden.*

up through pebbles to a nature-inspired pond that would be at home in a cottage-style garden. In between are formal ponds that can be round, rectangular, or even T-shaped.

Whatever your choice, the water should be kept moving to prevent it from becoming stagnant, and that means organizing a small pump to circulate and reuse the water. Submersible pumps can be placed at the bottom of ponds, and some wall masks come already fitted with a pump. You will also need to have electricity available where you want to site the water feature, so it is best to plan this before the garden is landscaped

LEFT: *This water feature has been planned as part of the garden architecture and is set within a brick-built arch on the wall, which has then been lined with pebbles for a rich texture.*

or paved. Electricity should always be installed by a qualified electrician.

Once the electricity is in position, putting in a pond is not beyond anyone who is handy around the house, especially if you use a ready-made liner. There is a choice of premolded fiberglass linings and the more easily disguised flexible butyl rubber or plastic sheeting. Once the liner is in position, you can cover the edges with rocks, pebbles, and clever planting.

It is best not to site the pond under overhanging branches because autumn leaves will fall into it, contaminating the pond as they decay.

If you have small children, opt for a water feature that does not form any depth of water (such as one that drains through pebbles) because a toddler can drown in just a few inches of water. Even if you want to plan a larger pool, you could always fill it with pebbles, letting the fountain splash over these until the children are older and the pebbles can be removed.

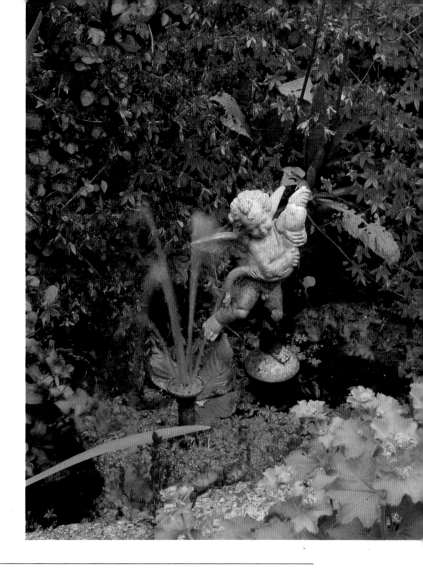

RIGHT: *An enchanting little pond, complete with fountain and cherub, mimics designs on a much grander scale.*

Miniature Pond

This delightful miniature pond, complete with waterlily, has been made in a glazed pot that adds an enchanting touch when "planted" in the herbaceous border.

TOOLS AND MATERIALS
Large, glazed ceramic pot, at least 15 in deep
Miniature waterlily

Choose a pot without a drainage hole. Partly fill with water. Put the waterlily still in its pot into the bottom. Then fill up with water.

Storage

Gardening brings with it an extraordinary amount of practical paraphernalia. Tools, pots, and planters, potting compost, raffia, string, seeds, and baskets are but a few of the bulky and space-consuming examples. For tools and equipment, garden sheds are the classic solution that most gardens can accommodate, though smaller gardens may be restricted to a mini-shed or tool shed, which can be as small as 12 in deep and so can be tucked into a corner. However, sheds can become an attractive part of the garden architecture if painted and decorated.

Another solution is to put your goods on show. Garden pots can be very visual and, displayed on

LEFT: *A pretty little wire shelving unit, intertwined with clematis, makes a delightful garden detail that serves a practical purpose too, providing storage for pots, string, pruning shears and wire.*

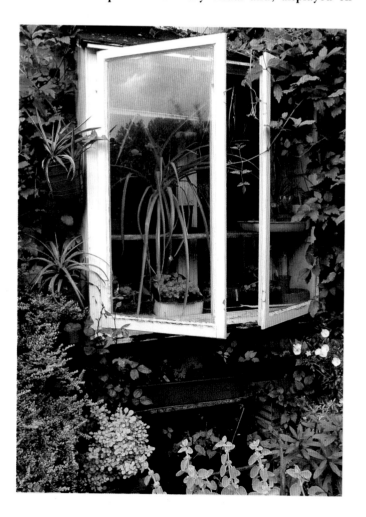

weatherproof shelves, can become part of the decorative appeal of the garden. This is an excellent solution for very small gardens and patios, which still need space for the practicals. Instead of buying ready-made garden shelving, you could build your own from timber and treat it with exterior-quality paint. Metal shelves can be given a new life using car spray paint or specially manufactured metal paint, which can even be sprayed straight over old rust. All shelves should be attached firmly to the garden wall – avoid attaching to the house wall since this could lead to water damage. Once fitted, use the shelves for displays, to store tools, or for bringing on young seedlings, which can look delightful planted in ranks of terracotta pots.

LEFT: *There was no room for a greenhouse or even a cold frame in this tiny 20-ft garden, so a "cabinet" was attached to the outside of the house window and given a pair of outward-opening windows. This solution provides perfect protection for young seedlings, which can be tended from inside as well as outside. Shelving underneath this outdoor glass cabinet makes a good second home for the young plants as they mature.*

ABOVE: *Old clay pots make a decorative corner display on a blue-painted plant stand.*

ABOVE: *Shelving can be used for purely decorative purposes outside as well as inside. Here, simple pebbles, arranged on a blue-painted shelf mounted on corbels, make a charming decorative detail in the garden.*

LEFT: *Bakery shelves make an attractive garden nursery for growing seedlings.*

Garden Furniture

Furnishing the garden gives you somewhere to sit and relax and, at the same time, adds to the architectural element. Some furniture, like traditional stone furniture, is designed to be an almost permanent part of the garden; certainly it is not meant to be moved often. Architecturally, it provides another step up, its legs almost representing balustrades. And while these wonderful garden fixtures aren't really within most people's price range, a similar role is played by old wooden garden benches which, as they weather to a soft green-tinged gray, take on a permanent air as part of the garden architecture.

Single benches exude a peaceful air, probably because they are not conducive to conversation but are more for sitting and contemplating. Love seats, designed in an S-shape, create a more sociable atmosphere since people sit facing each other. Tables and chairs represent social times in the garden, whether you are simply eating outside with the family, snacking with a friend, or having a party. Permanent outdoor furniture can be made of wood, metal, or plastic. Also decorative – and comfortable – outdoors, but not weatherproof, are wicker and Lloyd loom.

LEFT: *This delightful metal bench was given a new lease on life when it was painted a bright Mediterranean blue. The color works particularly well here, since it complements the marvelous cascades of purple wisteria.*

ABOVE: *This modern wrought-iron furniture takes reference from French styles of the nineteenth century, the elegant, lightweight lines of which are now enjoying another revival.*

LEFT: *Elaborate cast-iron furniture became very popular in Victorian times, and its popularity has not waned, though its price means you are more likely to see it in public places than in people's homes.*

RIGHT: *An old Lloyd loom chair was given a fresh look a few years ago with two shades of blue spray-on car paint. Even though the finish is now rather worn, the chair exudes a comfortable, cottagy feel.*

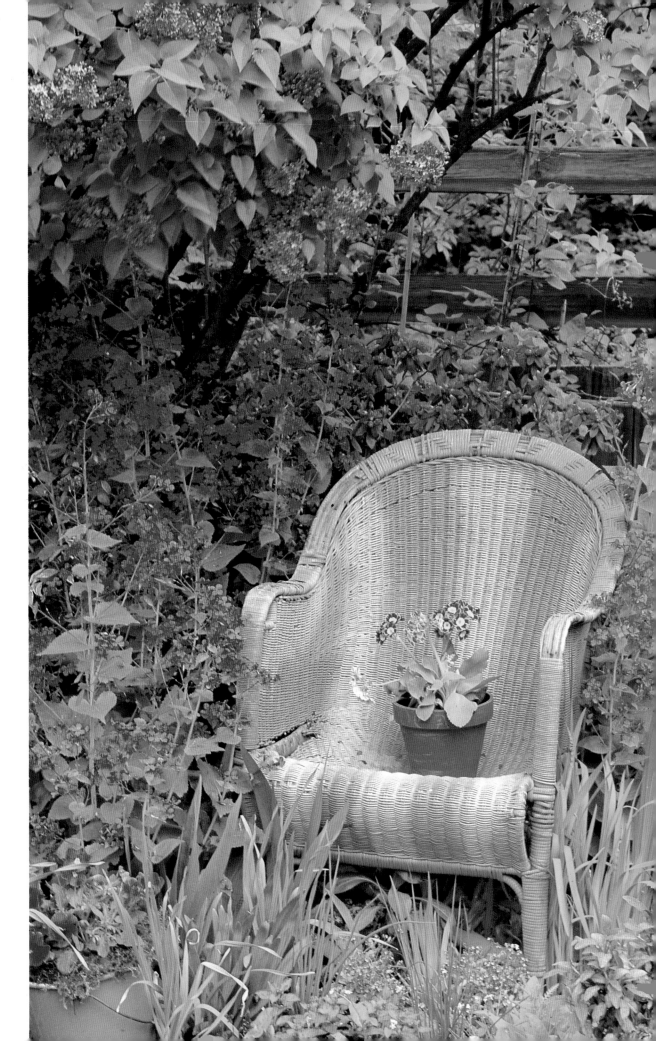

A Touch of Paint

Coordinating furniture with its surroundings helps to give the garden a harmonious ambience. By painting old furniture, you can keep the costs down because you can pick up bargain pieces from thrift shops or simply rejuvenate old kitchen chairs which are due for re-placement. You can also be sure of perfect blending since paints come in hundreds of shades. These two pairs of chairs were most unattractive when they were picked up: the slatted ones were peeling and the Tyrolean style were finished with a tired old varnish.

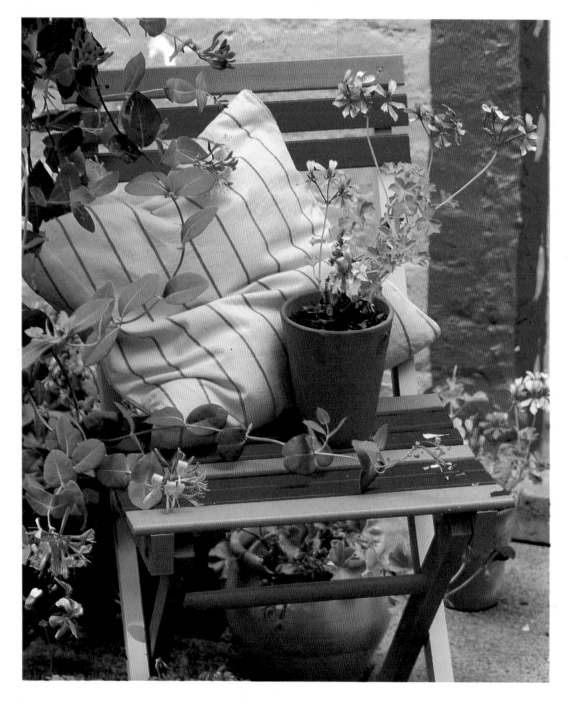

LEFT: *Clashing Caribbean colors in pink and tangerine make for a lively look in a brightly colored garden.*

ABOVE: *Taupe and white make an elegant combination for a chair that takes on Italian-style flair. It is an ideal finish for a garden that features a lot of the natural wooden tones.*

ABOVE RIGHT: *The shape of this chair is reminiscent of traditional Tyrolean design, so this has been enhanced by the choice of colors and decoration. These shades also naturally complement the colors of a summer garden.*

RIGHT: *The same chair is given a bright, modern finish to team with the painted shed wall behind. It also coordinates well with the silver-gray foliage and lipstick-pink flowers.*

Mosaic Garden Table

This striking mosaic table has been made from bits of broken old china pots and chipped decorative tiles, yet with clever color coordination and a simple, clear design, it makes the most attractive, weatherproof garden furniture around. Although it is resilient to dampness, bring it in during very rainy periods and over the winter.

PREPARATION

Draw the circle using a pair of compasses made from a piece of string tied to a drawing pin at one end and a pencil at the other. Push the drawing pin into the center of the plywood, making sure that the string is 2 ft long. Then draw the circle. Cut out using a jigsaw.

TOOLS AND MATERIALS

1 in plywood
    at least 4 × 4 ft
String
Pencil
Drawing pin
Jigsaw
Wood primer
Brush

Plenty of broken
    china
Tile cutters
Tile adhesive
Tile grout
Grout color,
    optional
Plastic gloves
Scrub brush

1 Draw the design on the plywood circle, adjusting the string length of the compasses to draw the concentric circles.

2 Prime the table with wood primer. Allow to dry according to the manufacturer's instructions.

3 Cut out pieces of china to fit the design, and try them out on the table top.

4 Mix the tile adhesive according to the manufacturer's instructions and "butter" it on to the "inside" of each piece of china before placing in position.

5 Once the design is complete, mix the grout and color, if color is desired. Wearing plastic gloves, use your fingers to work the grout in between all the china pieces. Using a scrub brush, continue to work the grout in. Then clean off any excess.

Garden Console Table

This indoor console table has been given an outdoor paint treatment for a whimsical touch in the garden. Accessorize it as an indoor end table, as here, or use it for drinks or serving dishes when entertaining outside.

TOOLS AND MATERIALS

Console table

Medium-grade sandpaper

White acrylic wood primer

2-in decorating brush

Masonry paint

Artist's acrylic paints in terracotta
  and pink

Small decorating brush

Fine masonry paint

Acrylic scumble glaze

Water for thinning

Cloth

Sheet of tracing paper

Pencil

Craft knife

Stencil cardboard

Stencil brush

Polyurethane varnish

1 Thoroughly sand all the surfaces. Prime with white acrylic wood primer. Allow to dry. Tint masonry paint with terracotta paint, and use as a primer. Allow to dry for four to six hours.

2 Tint fine masonry paint with pink acrylic paint and thin with scumble glaze and water. Paint on and rub off in the direction of the grain. Allow to dry.

3 Using the template at the back of the book, trace and cut a leaf stencil from cardboard. Using the terracotta paint, stencil leaves on to the table. Allow to dry. Then varnish.

Getting Comfortable

In summer, there is nothing more enjoyable than lounging around in the garden, and this is where the softer, more reclining types of furniture come in. The lounger is the lotus-eater's dream – more daybed than chair. Wood-slatted steamer chairs were the original loungers, designed for use on long voyages. Their modern-day equivalent – in wood, metal, or plastic – would be given an upholstered cushion. Hammocks are another kind of daybed and, gently swaying between a pair of trees, they would challenge anyone to stay awake. Other, softer "furniture" includes canvas types – deck chairs and director's chairs – and even thick, plaid picnic rugs and plastic-backed canvas cushions for getting comfortable on picnics.

RIGHT: *A hammock strung between two trees is perfect for whiling away lazy summer days.*

ABOVE: *Given a foot rest and, perhaps, a cushion, even wooden outdoor furniture can be truly relaxing. Add a trug of flowers on an end table for the lived-in feel.*

ABOVE: *This whimsical, plastic-covered, Louis XIV chair offers indoor comfort outside.*

Decorative Deck Chairs

There is little in the way of garden furniture to beat deck chairs. Their sheer loungeability, foldability and even refurbishability simply can't be beaten! You can buy striped chair canvases ready to nail on, but why not go a step or two further and add some pattern to a plain canvas? It really is not difficult, even if you have never considered yourself to be great with the paintbrush. One of these designs was made with a precut stencil, the other one was inspired by out-of-copyright bird motif designs, which are reproduced at the back of the book.

TOOLS AND MATERIALS
FOR THE "INDIAN BIRDS" DESIGN

Deck chair

5-ft length deck-chair canvas

Iron

Decorative outdoor woodstain for chair frame

Small decorating brush

Sheet of 16 × 12-in tracing paper

Soft and hard pencil

Soft fabric pens in red, green, purple, yellow, and blue

Ruler

Masking tape

White cloth

12 dome-headed upholstery tacks

TOOLS AND MATERIALS
FOR THE "STENCILED-RUG" DESIGN

Deck chair, canvas, and woodstain as for "Indian Birds" design

Iron

Small decorating brush

Precut stencil

Masking tape

Stencil brush

Stencil paints in red, ocher, olive, and aqua

White cloth

12 dome-headed upholstery tacks

"INDIAN BIRDS" DESIGN

Wash, rinse, dry, and iron the canvas to remove any dressing. Remove the old deck chair cover, and paint the frame with a decorative outdoor stain. Using the tracing paper, trace the bird motifs. Using a soft pencil, scribble densely on the back. Place this side down in the desired position on the canvas, and transfer the bird by drawing over the trace lines with a sharp pencil. You will probably then have to go over the lines again on the canvas. Using the soft fabric pens, color in the birds. For the border, measure ¾ in from each edge of the canvas, and place masking tape the full length of the canvas. Draw a wavy line down the full length. Then, using a contrasting pen, fill in the edges so a little canvas shows on both sides of the wavy line. Repeat for the inside borders, first placing masking tape on both sides of each border. When dry, set the ink by covering with a white cloth and pressing with the iron at its hottest setting, covering each part for at least two minutes. Use upholstery tacks to attach the canvas securely to the chair.

LEFT: *Woodstain, a length of vivid canvas, and some soft fabric pens are all you need to revitalize an old deck chair.*

"STENCILED-RUG" DESIGN

Prepare the canvas and the deck chair the same way as for the "Indian Birds" design. This design is made up of three motifs: the central motif, a tiny arrowhead, and a cross bordered by lines at the top and bottom. The cross-and-lines motif makes up the border, butted one up to the other. The arrowheads are positioned inside that and the three large motifs are placed in the center. Work out the areas of the design before you start. Starting with the borders, place the stencil in position using masking tape. Load the stencil brush with paint, and remove the excess by dabbing on a piece of newspaper until there is hardly any paint left on the brush. Apply this color to the relevant part of the stencil. Move the stencil, and repeat until all areas of that color have been painted. Using a fresh color, reposition the stencil over the original color and apply. Repeat until the design is complete. Set the paint and attach the canvas to the chair the same way as for the "Indian Birds" design.

LEFT: *Stenciling is a very quick way of creating a highly individual deck chair.*

ACCESSORIES AND DECORATIONS

When it comes to style, it is the details that count – the individual choice of decorations that express your personality. Be they large or small, these are the treats that add the finishing touches.

OPPOSITE: *Geraniums in clashing shades of bright red and pink are set off to perfection in a terracotta pot painted with stripes of vivid color.*

Outdoor Decorations

Sculpture is the classic outdoor art form. However, if either money to spend on garden decorations or space to display them is limited, then there are other alternatives. Anything that adds structure and form to the garden can be used. Flowerpots and containers can be part of the decorations. The traditional example is the classic urn. But you don't even have to go that far. Ordinary pots, painted or carefully arranged in groups, can make a statement, as can unusual containers. Think of some unusual hanging baskets such as a colander, basket, or bucket, or group potted plants into a spectacular container, such as an old wheelbarrow, to make a display.

You could choose more purely decorative ideas, such as pinwheels, wind chimes, driftwood, or pebble collections. Or you can fashion your own decorations – motifs such as hearts or stars made from twigs and branches, wire, or raffia.

LEFT: *This inexpensive, painted bamboo bird cage, filled with potted pinks, makes a simple yet charming ornament.*

ABOVE: *Even simple galvanized shapes take on decorative appeal when given a coat of paint.*

LEFT: *A merry group of drilled limpets hung on strong thread makes an attractive, joyous wind chime.*

OPPOSITE: *An old wicker mannequin teamed with a miniature wirework version make unexpected garden decorations.*

Hearts in the Garden

Hearts hold universal appeal, and there is no reason why they shouldn't find a home in the garden. You will be surprised by what you can make from the most rudimentary weatherproof materials. Garden wire, chicken wire, twigs, and raffia are all ideal. The beauty of the heart shape is that it is very easy to achieve. A circle of wire soon becomes a heart when the center is given a dip and the end a point. Twigs can be coaxed into curves to make two halves, then bound together top and bottom.

RIGHT: *A simple chicken-wire heart decorated and suspended with paper string makes a pretty decoration for a sheltered spot.*

ABOVE: *This heart-shaped wreath carries a seasonal message. The twig framework is wound around with variegated ivy and red berries, with a Christmas rose to finish.*

ABOVE: *A heart made from garden wire is given a more decorative texture by knotting natural raffia dyed green and ocher all around the shape.*

Wire Heart

This delightful filigree heart is not difficult to make from ordinary garden wire, and it is certainly robust enough to withstand a winter outside. It is composed of several smaller hearts bent into shape with ordinary, household pliers, then wired together in a beautiful all-over design. Make just one and hang it in a tree, or make several in different sizes or even from different wires. Then group them together on a wall or fence for a delightful display.

TOOLS AND MATERIALS

Wire cutters
Pliers
Medium-gauge garden wire
Florist's wire or fuse wire
Raffia for hanging

1 *Make several small heart shapes in various sizes by cutting short pieces of wire. Using the pliers, bend to a V-shape halfway along each piece and into a curl at both ends.*

2 *To make the large heart shape, cut two lengths of garden wire. Using the pliers, bend one piece into a curve for the top of the heart and form a loop at each end. Bend the second piece into a V-shape and form a loop at each end. Link the loops together to join the two pieces. Lay the small hearts inside the large one as you make them, until they fill the shape.*

3 *Using florist's or fuse wire, bind the smaller hearts to the large heart and to each other where they touch, until the whole ensemble is stable. Make a hanger from raffia.*

Garden Sculpture

The classic garden decoration is sculpture. For centuries, stone statues, busts, and fountains have graced formal and informal gardens, providing focal points at the end of vistas or charming finds in secluded spots. The classic Greek and Roman figures are still popular, along with baroque-style cherubs and putti (little boys). Originals in stone, aged by lichens, natural salts, and the passage of time, which highlight detail and combine to create a patina, are exquisite but usually prohibitively expensive. However, the aging process can be accelerated on modern stone versions by coating them with natural yogurt and keeping them in damp, shady places.

Beautiful as the traditional forms of sculpture are, there are alternatives that may be far more relevant to

LEFT: *A rusty wheel and mannequin's hand create a faintly sinister sculpture that is reflected in a mirror set against the garden wall. A tiny, diamond-shaped mirror hangs between, twisting, turning, and glinting in the sun to give the whole ensemble a dynamic quality.*

LEFT: *Metal and water provide a fascinating, moving sculpture that is a cross between a bird bath and a water feature.*

OPPOSITE: *An exquisite male torso, turned modestly toward the wall, provides art and structure to the side of a garden.*

your garden and far more personal to you. Metal and wire sculpture is fashionable today and works very well outside, as does willow, woven into dynamic figures. Mosaic, too, can be a lovely medium for sculpture as it quickly transforms all sorts of unpromising bits of paraphernalia.

Plants themselves can become sculpture, such as in topiary where, generally, small-leaved evergreens are clipped into spirals, cones, orbs, and animals. It is a long process since the shrubs take time to grow, but some garden centers sell them already started, and all you have to do is keep them trimmed to shape.

OPPOSITE: *Even a rusty old chair frame can become sculpture. This one, flanked on all sides by neatly trimmed trees, is given throne-like importance.*

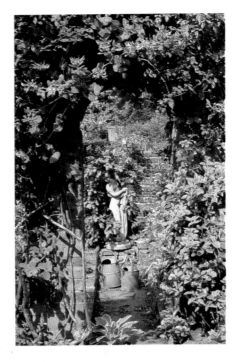

LEFT: *Classical-style statues make elegant focal points, set at the end of vistas.*

ABOVE: *Old galvanized baths and bowls have been whimsically decorated with ceramic chips cut from broken china, a couple of old teacups, and ginger-jar tops.*

ABOVE: *Evergreens clipped into simple topiary shapes make classic living sculptures that need not be overwhelming. Kept to a smaller scale in pots, they become enchanting details in any garden.*

Decorating Pots

Transforming an ordinary terracotta pot or simple galvanized bucket into something special really doesn't have to be difficult. There are so many media to choose from that it is an easy matter to find one that suits you. You may be happy with paint applied in bold geometric patterns or simple motifs. If you are more skilled you might like to try something a little more figurative. Another easy option is to stick small objects on to your pots – ceramic chips, for example, to make a mosaic or shells arranged in a simple, textural pattern.

OPPOSITE: *Simple patterns in coordinated ceramic chips make for striking mosaic garden pots.*

LEFT: *Plain terracotta pots painted in clear Mediterranean greens and blues and planted with scarlet geraniums and sweet-smelling thyme will enliven even the dullest corner of the garden or patio.*

ABOVE: *Terracotta pots color-washed in springtime shades of yellow and green are ideal for a display of daffodils and crocuses.*

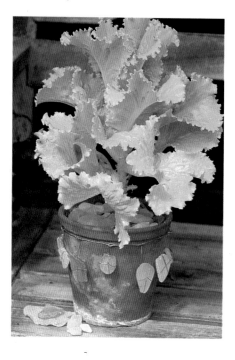

LEFT: *This pot has been given a necklace of weathered glass "beads" dangling on wires from a main wire attached under the rim of the pot.*

Mexican Painted Pots

A series of basic motifs painted over stripes of vibrant colors gives simple pots a rich Mexican look. It is lovely to let some of the untreated terracotta color show through, especially if you use pots with a fluted top like this one. Planted with geraniums in hot summer colors and stacked together, they make a lively garden feature.

TOOLS AND MATERIALS

Fluted-top garden pot

Masking tape

Scissors

White primer

Small decorating brush

Gouache poster colors

2 artist's brushes, one very fine

Polyurethane varnish

1 *Mark the stripes on the pot using masking tape. Cut some lengths into narrower widths to get variation in the finished design. Bear in mind that the areas covered by masking tape will remain natural terracotta.*

2 *Completely paint the main body of the pot with primer. Allow to dry according to the manufacturer's instructions.*

3 *Paint the colored stripes, changing the color after each band of masking tape. Allow the paint to dry completely.*

4 *Peel off the masking tape to reveal colored stripes alternating with terracotta stripes.*

5 *Using the fine artist's brush and the primer, paint simple motifs over the stripes. When completely dry, coat with varnish.*

Verdigris Bucket

TOOLS AND MATERIALS

Galvanized bucket

Medium-grade sandpaper

Metal primer

Small decorating brush

Gold paint

Large artist's brush

Amber shellac

Artist's acrylic paint in

white and aqua

Water for mixing

Natural sponge

Polyurethane varnish

1 Sand the bucket, then prime with metal primer. Allow to dry for two to three hours. Paint with gold paint, and allow to dry for two to three hours.

2 Paint with amber shellac and allow to dry for 30 minutes. Mix white acrylic paint with aqua-green and enough water to make a watery consistency.

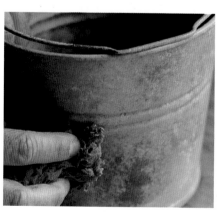

3 Sponge the verdigris paint on, and allow to dry for one to two hours. Apply a coat of varnish.

There is something irresistible about the luminous, blue-green tones of verdigris. It is a color that always complements plants and is not difficult to reproduce on a cheap, galvanized bucket. To make the rust bucket shown behind the verdigris one, follow the steps below, but substitute rust-colored acrylic paint for the aqua.

Lead Chimney

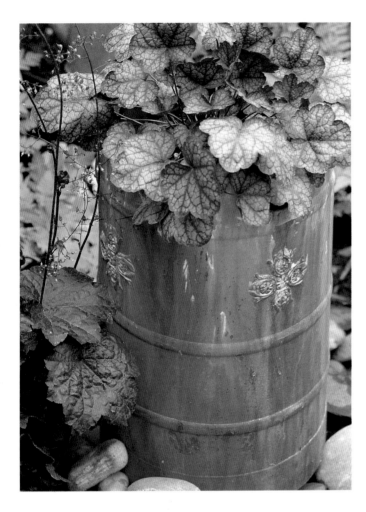

The wonderful chalky tones of lead have made it a popular material for garden containers down the centuries. But lead is incredibly heavy and very expensive, so here is a way of faking it. Use a plastic, terracotta-colored chimney and some simple paint effects.

TOOLS AND MATERIALS

Plastic, terracotta-colored
  chimney

Sandpaper

Acrylic primer

Large artist's brush

Charcoal-gray latex paint

Acrylic scumble glaze

White latex paint

Water

Decorating brush

Polyurethane varnish

1 Sand the chimney to give it a key. Paint with one coat of acrylic primer, and allow to dry for one to two hours.

2 Apply one coat of charcoal-gray latex paint and allow to dry for two hours.

3 Tint the scumble glaze with white latex paint and thin with water. Paint over the chimney randomly. Wash over with water and allow to dry.

4 Add more of the white scumble mixture to parts of the chimney for extra color and "age." Varnish with polyurethane varnish.

Functional Decorations

The very paraphernalia of gardens can be decorative. An old garden fork, its handle polished with use, a galvanized watering can, turned soft gray with time, or a wheelbarrow, pitted with wear, all have attractive forms that give structure to the garden. Somehow, the balance and symmetry necessary for tools to be efficient at their job usually also result in shapes that are easy on the eye. They have reassuring associations, too. They remind us that people are nearby. So let them loiter around the garden and leave them where they were last used, and they will reward you with their ever-changing decorative appeal.

ABOVE: *Sundials may not be movable decorations, but their original* raison d'être *reminds us that these are not fripperies. They were clearly more necessary in centuries gone by than they are today, but they still exude a functional quality that is honest and pleasing.*

LEFT: *Even old garden tools make decorative garden ornaments left just where they were last used.*

LEFT: *An old watering can, its curves reminiscent of a vintage car, provides a simple structure left by the garden bed.*

Twigwam

Plant supports are functional – but that doesn't mean they can't be decorative, too. This one, made from branches pruned from garden trees interwoven with willow, makes a charming structural detail in the flower beds or it can be used to support clematis or any other climber for a wonderful, free-standing, outdoor floral display.

TOOLS AND MATERIALS

3 unbranched poles, about 3 ft long

String or willow for tying

3 unbranched poles, 12 in long

Plenty of fine, freshly cut willow branches

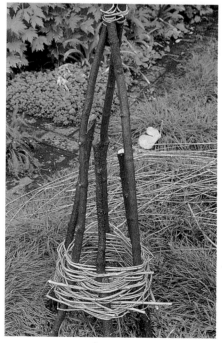

1 *Stand the three taller poles up to form a "wigwam," and tie them together at the top with string or willow.*

2 *Stand the three shorter poles between the longer ones, and tie them in the same way. Start to weave the willow branches in and out of all the poles, working upward from the bottom.*

3 *Once enough of the wigwam has been woven to keep the shorter poles securely in position, untie the top fastening. Continue weaving until the shorter poles are almost covered.*

Chicken-wire "Cloche"

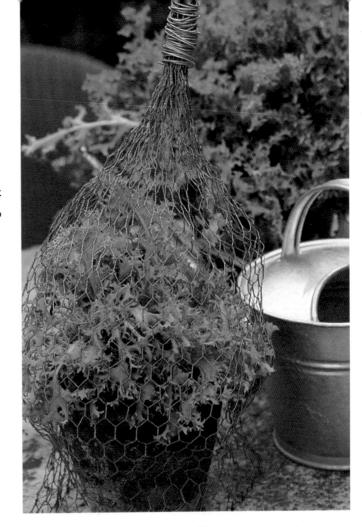

This quirky chicken-wire "cloche" can be used to protect plants from slugs and birds, or can simply be "planted" into the flower bed as a charming and original miniature obelisk.

TOOLS AND MATERIALS

Wire cutters

Fine-mesh chicken wire

Pliers

Medium-gauge garden wire

1 *Using the wire cutters, cut a piece of chicken wire about 20 × 20 in. Roll it to form a tube, making sure the twisted sides of each lozenge shape run vertically. Join the tube by twisting the cut ends of the wire around each other, using either your fingers – with care – or the pliers, whichever you find easier.*

2 *Use the pliers to squeeze together each lozenge shape. At the top, to 3 in from the top, squeeze each lozenge as tightly as it will go. Then continue to pinch the holes down the tube, allowing the holes to become larger and larger until the fullest part has been reached. At the bottom end, make a "skirt" by squeezing the lozenges.*

3 *Wind garden wire tightly around the top of the cloche to finish.*

Pretty Effects for Practical Areas

Vegetable patches don't have to be the Cinderellas of the garden. There is something voluptuous about burgeoning fruits and first-class vegetables, and there is something appealing about the structures they need to climb up. So make a virtue of your vegetables, whether you plan to give them their own special space or let them fraternize with the flowers.

LEFT: There is something appealing about pea sticks, in that the twiggy branches give the appearance of a wild hedgerow up which the peas are scrambling. There is a practical element, too: the twigs offer plenty of climbing support.

LEFT: Soldier-like bamboo canes take on an even more regimental appearance with their labels tied uniformly along the line.

ABOVE: Keeping track of plant labels can be nearly impossible once the plants are growing and overflowing their original sites, so turn them into a decoration in themselves. Cut out a board from plywood, giving it a decorative motif at the top, such as these tulips. Paint it in bright colors, screw in some hooks, and you have an attractive garden record of what you have planted.

OPPOSITE: Whether it is fruit, vegetables, or seedlings you want to protect, make a whimsical scarecrow to double as an amusing garden sculpture. This dapper chap with hand-tool hands and a colander face, wears a sporty Panama hat.

Chicken-box Plant Stand

It is fun, especially in spring when the plants are low, to hoist a few flowers on high. And here is an unusual way to achieve that. Make a decorative chicken nesting on a box, raise it on a stake, and fill the box with pots of seasonal flowers. Use it to bring color to any patchy part of the garden, wherever that may be as the year progresses.

TOOLS AND MATERIALS

Sheet of 16 × 12-in tracing paper

Soft pencil

Sheet of 16 × 12-in paper

Scissors

MDF (medium-density fiberboard),
    measuring about 2 × 2 ft

Jigsaw

1-in plywood, measuring at
    least 30 × 18 in

6 screws

Screwdriver

Primer

Small decorating brush

Model-painting enamel in red, orange,
    white, blue, black, and green

Artist's brush

2 × 3-in post, about
    4 ft long

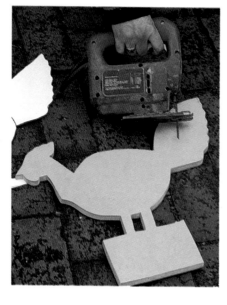

1 Using the template at the back of the book, make a paper pattern for the chicken. Draw around the chicken shape on the MDF. Cut out, using a jigsaw. Cut three pieces of plywood measuring 6¾ × 3½ in and one measuring 6¾ × 2in.

2 Screw the larger panels on to the chicken, one on each side. Screw the narrower, bottom panel between them. Screw the final plywood panel on to the front.

3 Paint both sides of the chicken and the box with primer. Allow to dry according to the manufacturer's instructions.

4 Sketch the chicken details on to both sides of the chicken shape and, using model-painting enamel, add the colors. Allow to dry overnight.

5 Paint the box green. Allow to dry for three hours. Screw the post to the back of the box.

LIVING IN
THE GARDEN

The real joy of a garden is to be able to relax
outside with friends and family in your own
private outdoor room. With space to entertain,
play, or do nothing the garden will be
ready for you whenever you feel like a
breath of fresh air.

OPPOSITE: *A miniature garden room in
itself, an awning is invaluable when the
sun is hot, the weather is gusty, or if your
garden lacks privacy.*

Comfortable Living Areas

If you set up a comfortable living area in the garden, you are much more likely to use it. With table and chairs standing ready, it is so much easier to bring the coffee and rolls out for breakfast al fresco. With an area set aside for the children, they will much more readily run outside to play. The priority is to earmark a sheltered living area with a cozy, room-like feel. If it is not next to the house, it will need to be screened by hedges or trellis to lend a sense of privacy. You don't need a large space. Just think how cramped some restaurants are and yet, once seated, you feel comfortable. Once the living area is established, try to incorporate something that stimulates each of the senses. Place a pretty plant within view of the seating area or position the chairs to look on to a pleasant vista. Nature will offer plenty to please your ear: summer bird song, the hum of bees, and the whisper of trees and shrubs gently stirred by a breeze can be enhanced by the music of wind chimes, and a water feature can offer the relaxing sound of trickling water.

For fragrance, site plants with richly perfumed blooms near the seating area. Old-fashioned roses and honeysuckle are hard to beat, or try aromatic lavender and rosemary. Many flowers exude their scent at night. Summer jasmine and tobacco plants (nicotiana) are two favorites. For touch, you can plant a contrast of textures from feathery love-in-a-mist and shapely ferns to rich succulents. Finally, taste can be stimulated by nearby aromatic herbs or fragrant fruits such as strawberries and blackberries.

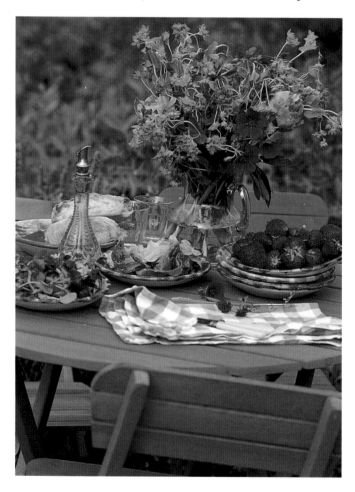

ABOVE: *Having lunch outside in the summer can be a memorable occasion. Attractive garden furniture and a pretty wild flower arrangement create a restful ambience, while fresh fruits and salads look wonderful on colorful china.*

ABOVE: *Throw a blue-checked cloth over the garden table, add some seasonal potted arrangements, and you have the perfect setting for enjoying drinks outside, even on a cool but sunny spring day.*

ABOVE: *Swathes of roses on a trellis at the back and over archways on each side provide a fragrant and intimate screen for a picturesque seating area.*

LEFT: *Part of the enjoyment of being outside is having a view to admire. This seating area on the patio next to the house overlooks an almost classical vista in an urban garden.*

Awnings and Umbrellas

Living outside sometimes requires shelter and shade, be it from the wind or a blistering sun. On a windy day, a windbreak of some kind will enable you to sit outside even in early spring or early autumn, when it would otherwise be impossible. A capacious sun umbrella, on the other hand, will allow you to dine outside or simply relax under its shelter even in the middle of a hot summer's day.

RIGHT: A dead tree provided the inspiration for a sheltered seating area in this garden. The natural awning was constructed from the pruned branches, while a dovecote on the top introduces the gentle cooing of doves.

ABOVE: Take two chairs and one umbrella, and you immediately have a pleasantly informal seating arrangement and a movable sheltered spot from which to enjoy the garden.

ABOVE: Late summer jobs, such as topping and tailing fruit, become pleasurable pastimes under an awning. Original Edwardian awnings like this one come with a lightweight metal frame that is easily erected, and the awning is simply slipped over.

Wind Chime

The charm of this shell wind chime lies in its simplicity. Garden ornaments need to be visually striking since they will be viewed from some distance. In this case, the sand dollars give the wind chime its striking form while the cockle shells strung on raffia provide the music.

TOOLS AND MATERIALS

Raffia

Scissors

10 predrilled cockle shells

Electric drill with fine drill bit (if you cannot get predrilled shells)

3 sand dollars

1 *Cut three lengths of raffia about 2 ft long and two 18 in long. If you can get predrilled cockle shells, so much the better, if not, carefully drill each shell using an electric drill with a fine drill bit. Tie one shell to each end of each length of raffia. Fold all the lengths of raffia in half, and gather them together at the halfway point. Thread this loop through the hole in one sand dollar.*

2 *Feed the ends of the raffia, including the shells, through the loop to tie them to the sand dollar.*

3 *Feed two further lengths of raffia through the hole in the sand dollar, and tie them together at the top. In the same way, link and tie the other two sand dollars to the top of the chime.*

Children's Areas

In family homes, gardens are very much for the children. They need their own outdoor space to play in and, where there isn't enough room to run or kick a ball, the best solution is to set aside one area of the garden and build some sort of structure especially for them. They may like a playhouse, which provides all-weather outdoor play, or they may prefer a climbing frame or a swing and slide. If any of these are well planned, they need not take up too much space. If you are lucky enough to have a suitable tree, you may even be inspired to build a tree house, which wouldn't take up any space at all!

ABOVE: *Playhouses can be decorated to enhance the whole garden. They not only offer a private place for imaginative play in the early years and a den as the children get older, but they also provide ideal storage space for bulkier, favorite toys such as free-standing kitchens and doll houses.*

RIGHT: *These steps up to a platform take children to an exciting slide. The same idea could be adapted for a tree house.*

RIGHT: *A delightful, little crooked house, complete with veranda and chimney, is built on stilts with a short stairway leading up to it. The very stuff of nursery stories. Many an hour can be whiled away here in imaginative play.*

BELOW: *Climbing frames made from rustic poles blend happily into the garden. Carefully designed, they can be added to over the years should space allow, or simply adapted to keep the challenge fresh.*

Animal Friends

Even in the densest urban areas, the outdoors is not devoid of wildlife. Countless creatures consider our gardens to be their home, as much as we consider them a part of ours. Many creatures we very much welcome, delighting in watching their activities. And, of course, wild creatures often help to maintain the ecological balance, eating unwanted guests such as flies and other garden pests.

Most wild creatures like to be self-catering and are very happy to organize their own homes, though with a little encouragement, such as the provision of a shallow dish of fresh water, they will appreciatively settle on your plot. Some plants attract beneficial insects such as butterflies and bees. The most obvious ones are the more highly scented species such as buddleia (butterfly bush), lavender, and honeysuckle. Birds can be encouraged by bird feeders in the winter and bird baths in the summer. Toads, which are consummate devourers of flies, like to set up house in cool, damp places – in flowerpots laid on their sides in a leafy, private place, for instance, or under a pile of stones. Once in residence, they will stay, gradually working their way through the insect population.

BELOW: *Butterflies can be attracted into the garden by planting their favorite nectar-rich shrubs, such as buddleia and this exquisite pink autumn-flowering sedum.*

ABOVE: *Carefully positioned to catch the mellow afternoon sun, a leafy arbor can become a favorite spot for the resident cat.*

ABOVE: *A dovecote is not only architecturally pleasing, it provides a home for one of the most beautiful species of birds. And they don't even demand to live in the country. These doves moved into a bird house in a tiny town terrace.*

LEFT: *Bird baths can take the form of a piece of sculpture. This mosaic structure "nests" in a bed of marigolds and wallflowers.*

Lighting Effects

Enjoying the garden after nightfall is dependent on garden lighting and, in most domestic gardens, that is sadly lacking. If you are having your garden landscaped, you may consider having electricity cables laid and bringing in an expert to work out a proper plan. This would usually include general lighting, plus perhaps some spotlighting for focal points such as a favorite piece of statuary. But even if you don't want to go to that expense, there is a lot you can do.

Before you start, it is worth bearing in mind that, unless you are planning powerful floodlighting, you are unlikely to achieve the light levels you would normally expect inside. And would you want to? Part of the appeal of being outside at night is the moody lighting and the appreciation of the moon and stars.

The easiest solution for general outdoor lighting is to attach a powerful halogen light to the side of the house. Since the living areas of the garden are usually near the house, this should be ample. Another easy idea is to have an electrician fit an all-weather socket to the outside of the house, taking a spur off the ring main. This can then be used for plugging in both light and sound for fabulous evening entertainment. For special occasions, you may like to hire all-weather strings of lights to hang in the trees. Plain white bulbs are always particularly effective.

ABOVE: *Place outdoor lights under plants with strong architectural shapes to create drama in the garden at night.*

RIGHT: *Outdoor fairy lights woven into the trellis and climber make a charming decorative effect for summer evenings.*

OPPOSITE: *Spotlights highlighting the statuary and pond provide excellent outdoor lighting for this formal Italianate garden.*

Candle Power

Candles must surely offer the most romantic outdoor lighting. The light they cast is natural, flattering, and evocative of campfires. They are also very practical for outside as they don't rely on electricity. There are many forms of candle light. Ordinary indoor candles can simply be taken outside, candelabra and all, for a candle-lit dinner. If the weather is a bit breezy, use a lantern or some other holder which protects the flame from the elements. Choose lanterns that can take a substantial-sized candle, otherwise you will be forever jumping up and down to light yet another. Also, check that the metal work is strong since some imported aluminum lanterns collapse once the lit candle melts the solder holding them together.

As well as lanterns, you could try Victorian night-lights, tumbler-like glass containers that hang on wires, huge glass hanging lanterns, or candles in garden pots or galvanized buckets which, once they burn down below the rim, are protected from the wind. Candles that are specially designed to cope with the outside elements are garden flares, which produce a huge flame and can burn for up to three hours. The light they give off is also surprisingly bright, which makes them ideal for general lighting around the entertainment area or for pathway lighting.

The main danger of outdoor candles and garden flares is that the wind does blow the flame, so it is important always to position them well away from any foliage or furniture.

BELOW: *Lanterns provide perfect garden candle light since they protect the flame from the wind.*

ABOVE: *Garden flares, "planted" around the garden, provide a surprising amount of light. Many are also scented to discourage insects.*

ABOVE: *Victorian nightlights hung on wires create a romantic glow in the trees.*

RIGHT: *A large, glass hanging lantern makes enchanting lighting for dinner al fresco. Lotus-like flower candles float above a bed of shells, looking like an exotic lily pond.*

Gilded Candle Pots

Ordinary terracotta pots, gilded and filled with candle wax, offer the most enchanting outdoor lighting. Make several pots in assorted sizes to group on tables, patios, walls, and outdoor shelves.

TOOLS AND MATERIALS

Assorted terracotta pots

Red oxide primer

Small decorating brush

Water-based gold size

Gold Dutch metal leaf

Soft cloth

Amber shellac

Artist's acrylic paint in white
   and aqua

Water for mixing

Artist's brush

Wick

Candle wax

Double boiler

1 Prime each pot with red oxide primer. Allow to dry for three to four hours.

2 Apply a coat of water-based gold size, and allow to dry for about 30 minutes or until the size becomes transparent.

3 To apply the gold Dutch metal leaf, lift the sheets carefully and lay them on to the size, gently smoothing each one with a cloth or soft-bristled brush. Brush off any excess leaf, and polish with a soft cloth.

4 Apply a coat of amber shellac to seal the metal leaf, and allow to dry for 30 minutes.

5 To age the pots, tint a little white acrylic with aqua and thin with water, brush on, and rub off with a cloth. Allow to dry for two to three hours. For the candle, suspend the wick in the pot by tying it to a pole laid across the pot. Make sure the wick reaches the bottom of the pot. Slowly melt the wax in a double boiler, and pour into the pot. Allow to set overnight.

Entertaining Outside

What a joy it is, when all is said and done, to invite friends over and relax together in the garden. It is the wonderful casualness of al fresco eating that is so appealing. The food can be simple: fresh salads, fruits, and vegetables, served with just a little dressing or cream, whichever is appropriate. Meat or fish can simply be grilled or barbecued with fresh herbs, the aroma complementing the scent of the herbs growing in the beds. Add some bread, a bottle of wine, and you have all the ingredients for a memorable day or evening.

Decorating the table can be effortless. All you need is a table centerpiece of flowers and plants from the garden, and candles for an evening party.

BELOW: With all the gentle outdoor sounds plus the perfume of evening-scented flowers, even the simplest of informal gatherings becomes a special occasion.

ABOVE: Cocktail hour, when the heat of the day is over, is a wonderful time to get together in the garden, whether for entertainment or to celebrate bringing in the fruit harvest.

Iron Lantern

Give new aluminum lanterns the more appealing appearance of aged iron. Even the simplest shapes and brashest finishes become infinitely more pleasing when given the well-worn look of an antique lantern.

TOOLS AND MATERIALS

Masking tape

Metal lantern

Medium-grade sandpaper

White metal primer

Large artist's brush

Silver paint

Small natural sponge

Black latex paint

Red oxide artist's acrylic
    paint

Water for mixing

Flower mister

Satin polyurethane varnish

1 *Stick masking tape on to all the glass areas of the lantern. Sand the metal to provide a key. Paint one coat of metal primer on to all the metal parts of the lantern. Allow to dry for two to three hours. Paint on a silver base coat.*

2 *Dip the natural sponge into black latex paint and dab on to the lantern. Allow to dry for one to two hours.*

3 *Mix red oxide acrylic paint with a little water and, using the artist's brush, drip this down the lantern at intervals, to resemble rust. Spray with a flower mister. Allow to dry for one to two hours. Varnish, allow to dry, and remove the masking tape.*

Table Centerpieces

Outdoor table decorations are the very easiest to put together because they are at their most successful when they complement their surroundings. So plunder the garden, and then combine the ingredients with flair. You may cut a few flowers, add foliage or even fruit and vegetables or you may simply gather together some of the smaller pots from around the garden. The concentration on a table of what grows in naturally looser arrangements throughout the garden serves to focus the overall look.

ABOVE: *Ivy planted in glass-shaped galvanized containers and accessorized with a couple of pastel-painted canes to resemble straws makes a whimsical, cocktail centerpiece.*

LEFT: *In summer, a couple of potted strawberry plants are transformed into a centerpiece when they are contained in a wire jug and accessorized with a few ripe fruit.*

RIGHT: *A wire basket interwoven with raffia on its base gathers together pots of verbena surrounded by tiny pots of variegated ivy. The end result is an outdoor casualness perfectly in accord with its surroundings.*

BELOW: *Ornamental cabbages, complemented by individual cabbage leaves used decoratively on the napkins, and a miniature arrangement in a baby jar, make an unusually attractive centerpiece.*

Practicalities

Bringing color into the garden with paints and stains lends impact both to the planting and to the whole garden. You can do this by painting or staining fences, trellis work, garden buildings, furniture, and containers. However, any outdoor paint job has to be able to withstand a lot of beating from the weather, such as frosts, strong winds, torrential rain and the blistering summer sun. For this reason, it is best to use exterior-quality products. They are less likely to peel and flake, their colors are less likely to fade and they are specifically designed to protect the surface they are covering. Alternatively, you can achieve a reasonably hard-wearing finish using a wider variety of paints over a primer, then finishing with a polyurethane varnish when decorating items such as pots and containers, which are not crucial to the garden structure.

Whatever you plan to paint or stain, it is important to use compatible primers and varnishes, otherwise they may react against each other. So if you plan to use

ABOVE: *Gilded miniature clay pots, filled with candle wax, will add color and atmosphere to the garden room.*

a water-based product, make sure you also prime and finish using water-based products. Acrylics should be kept together and oil-based products should be kept together. Also, ideally, you should stick to one manufacturer's products for each job since that will guarantee compatibility. When you are not able to do this, it would be wise to test a small, hidden area, first.

Always do any kind of exterior painting on a dry, warm day, and preferably after several similar days, with the prospect of more to come. The reasons for this are clear. If the surface to be painted is damp, the paint will peel. If the surface is hot, from baking sun, it will blister. If there is a frost, it will "lift" the paint.

Remember, too, that several thin layers of paint always produce a more enduring and better-looking finish than one thick one.

LEFT: *Wonderful decorative effects can be created using just a few special materials, such as latex paint and acrylic paint, water-based gold size and Dutch metal leaf, gilt cream and felt-tipped pens in gold and silver.*

Tools for Painting

You will achieve a more controlled and permanent paint finish if you use the right tools for the job. And, if you are investing in new brushes, it makes sense to care for them by cleaning them correctly.

DECORATING BRUSHES

These are the best brushes to use for applying paint. For very large, flat surfaces you may need a latex paintbrush, but for most tasks a flat brush of around 3–4 in would be adequate. Sash brushes, so called because they are used to paint window frames, are around 1–2 in wide and are indispensable for many of the more difficult jobs.

TOOLS FOR PAINT EFFECTS

Artist's brushes are useful for creating the more decorative finishes, such as stone, lead, and verdigris paint effects. The finer the job, the finer the brush needs to be. Where the lines between one color and the next need to be merged, the paint should be applied with a natural sponge. To stipple paint, use a special stippling brush or a fine decorating sash brush. For stenciling, you will need a stencil brush which has short, stiff bristles. The brush should be used with a dabbing rather than a brushing action to prevent paint seeping under the stencil and spoiling the shape.

CLEANING UP

Brushes used for water-based products can be cleaned using soap and water. Work up a lather right up into the ferrule. Rinse thoroughly until the water runs clear. Squeeze and shake out any excess water, straighten the bristles, then lay on a piece of newspaper. Fold the paper to make a package around the bristles, which will restore them to shape and absorb excess moisture. Brushes used for oil-based products should be cleaned using white spirit. Wash out the white spirit using soap and water and dry as above.

LEFT: *(From left to right) stenciling brush, dusting brush (sometimes used for stippling paint surfaces), sash brush, softening brush (used to soften brush strokes before the paint dries), stippling brush, large decorating brush, rubber rocker (used to create wood-grain effects), artist's brushes, flat-bristle varnishing brush, natural sponge, soft cloth.*

Preparation Pays

Whatever job you are doing, make sure the surface is properly prepared first, following the manufacturer's instructions. There are various surface materials in the garden, all of which need different treatments. If you are retreating any surface, you should use the same type of product. For example, you won't be able to paint over oiled furniture or creosoted wood.

MASONRY

Prepare walls by removing dirt and loose paint with a stiff brush. If the wall is still powdery, seal the surface with a stabilizing solution.

Paint with smooth or textured masonry paint. This is available in hundreds of colors, most of which have to be mixed up specially by the supplier. If you want to use only a small amount, for decorative detailing or, perhaps, a shed wall, you can tint the paint with artist's color. Check a small amount first.

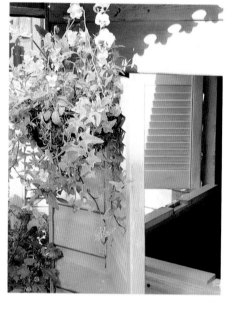

LEFT: *Garden sheds or playhouses made of smooth-planed wood can be painted with exterior-quality paints for a fresh, new finish.*

LEFT: *Old wooden furniture, such as deck chairs, can be given a new lease of life with a coat of colored wood stain.*

LEFT: *Using masonry paint tinted with artist's colors, exterior house walls can be as vibrant as you wish.*

SMOOTH-PLANED WOOD

Garden doors, garden furniture, and some garden buildings such as playhouses and sheds are made from smooth-planed wood. There are three types of products you can use to paint these: exterior gloss, exterior wood stain, and exterior varnish, which comes in a clear, matte or glossy finish and in a choice of colors. Most wood stains come in wood colors, though some specialty manufacturers produce colored stains, too. Outdoor buildings and furniture are usually bought pretreated with a preservative which you can paint over. However, check this before you buy. Wash the surface with a sugar soap solution, then rinse thoroughly. Rub down with wet and dry paper. Allow to dry out thoroughly. Then paint on a coat of exterior primer. Allow to dry, then rub down and apply a primer. Allow to dry, then rub down and apply exerior gloss paint. Always allow adequate drying time between each stage, taking the manufacturer's specified time as the absolute minimum.

If you would prefer a finish which allows the grain of the wood to show through, you can choose either a wood stain or a varnish. The color in wood stains penetrates the wood. Varnish, even if it is a stained varnish, sits on top. There is usually a complementary basecoat for use with these products.

ROUGH-SAWN WOOD

Most garden fencing, trellis, and some garden buildings are made of rough-sawn wood. These need to be treated with a staining product that soaks into the wood, rather than sits on top of it, as a paint or varnish does. Always check that the product is suitable for exterior, rough-sawn wood. Most of them come in a wood color or green, though some specialty manufac-

turers produce colored stains. Rough-sawn products are often pretreated with a preservative when you buy them. Check that the preservative can be painted over. If the product has not been preserved, use a compatible preservative before coating with stain.

METAL

Metal gates and railings can be painted with exterior-quality gloss paint. Brush previously painted metal with a wire brush to clean it and remove any loose paint and metal badly eroded by rust. Then dust off. Treat rust with a rust cure, and prime any new or bare metal with the appropriate metal primer, then allow to dry before applying the top coat. There are also special metal paints available in aerosol and brush-on versions that can be applied straight over the metal without priming, even if rusty. However, remove any loose rust first with a wire brush.

LEFT: *Garden trellis work doesn't have to be a uniform brown. Here, a soft-blue wood stain offers the perfect backdrop for a pink planting scheme.*

RIGHT: *Treat metal gates and railings to a new coat of exterior gloss or metal paint.*

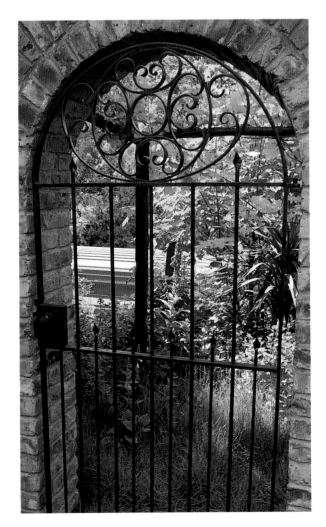

Templates

Unless indicated otherwise, all the templates and plans are drawn to actual size. To enlarge a template to the correct size, either use a grid system or a photocopier. For the grid system, trace the template and draw a grid of evenly spaced squares over your tracing. To scale up, draw a larger grid on to another piece of paper. Copy the outline on to the second grid by taking each square individually and drawing the relevant part of the outline in the equivalent larger square. To make templates you will need tracing paper, hard and soft pencils, paper or cardboard and scissors.

Pretty Pebble Rug page 30

Design plan

Ideas with Paint, pages 48/9

Leaf motif

Lemon and lime motif

Lizard motif

Enlarge by 200% for actual size

Customized Playhouse, pages 88/89

Fascia template

Garden Console Table, page 100

Leaf motif

Chicken-box Plant Stand, pages 126/127

Enlarge by 200% for actual size

Decorative Deck Chairs, pages 102/103

"Indian Birds" motifs

Stockists and Suppliers

UNITED STATES

Exterior masonry paints, gloss paints, stains, varnishes as well as concrete, granite and concrete stone pavings can be found in large, general hardware stores and home-improvement centers

Alsto's Handy Helpers
P.O. Box 1267
Galesburg, IL 61401
Tel: (800) 447–0048
Cedar patio furniture and swings, metal lawn chairs, gliders – catalog available

Ballard Designs
1670 DeFoor Avenue, NW
Atlanta, GA 30318–7528
Tel: (404) 351–5099
Cast architectural ornaments, metal and glass chairs, benches and tables – catalog available

Bamboo Fencer
31 Germania Street
Jamaica Plain, MA 02130
Tel: (800) 775–8641
Bamboo fencing of original and Japanese design – catalog available

Bufftech
2525 Walden Avenue
Buffalo, NY 14225
Tel: (800) 333–0579
Vinyl fencing made to resemble wood – catalog available

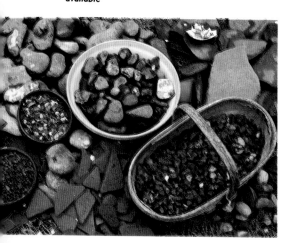

The Clapper Company
1121 Washington Street
West Newton, MA 02165
Tel: (617) 244–7900
Composting equipment and organic fertilizers as well as tools, garden ornaments and furniture

Country Casual
17317 Germantown Road
Germantown, MD 20874–2999
Tel: (301) 540–0040
Trellises and teak furniture – catalog available

Crescent Bronze Powder Co.
3400 N. Avondale Ave.
Chicago, IL 60618
Tel: (312) 529–2441
Metallic pigment colors including gold shades, metallic paints and lacquer

Discount Pond Supplies
P.O. Box 423371H
Kissimmee, FL 34742–3371
Fax: (407) 932–4019
Complete line of water garden supplies – free catalog available

Dorothy Biddle Service
P.O. Box 900
Greeley, PA 18425
Tel: (717) 226–3239
Preservatives, foams, floral clays, foam, picks, pins, wire, tapes, snips, beach pebbles, marble chips, moss, and adhesive. Also garden tools and accessories

Elizabeth Street
210 Elizabeth Street
New York, NY 10012
Tel: (212) 941–4800
Fountains and outdoor and garden objects – catalog available

Florentine Craftsmen, Inc.
46–24 28th Street
Long Island City, NY 11101
Tel: (718) 937–7632
Fountains, garden statuary, and furniture – catalog available

French Wyres
P.O. Box 131655
Tyler, TX 75713
Tel: (903) 597–8322
Trellis, urns, wire plant stands, and topiary frames – catalog available

Garden Accents
4 Union Hill Road
Conshohocken, PA 19428
Tel: (215) 825–5525
Antique and modern garden ornaments, statuary, lighting, stone and metal urns – catalog available

Garden Concepts
P.O. Box 241233
Memphis, TN 38124–1233
Tel: (901) 756–1649
Furniture, structures and accessories in wood – catalog available

Gardener's Eden
100 North Point Street
San Francisco, CA 94133
Tel: (800) 822–9600
Garden ornaments, metal, twig and wicker garden furniture

Hens & Feathers & Company
10 Balligomingo Road
Gulph Mills, PA 19428
Tel: (800) 282–1910
Urns, planters, fountains, and statuary made from bonded marble resin in hand-finished patinas – catalog available

Kenneth Lynch & Sons
P.O. Box 488
Wilton, CT 06897
Tel: (203) 762–8363
Composting equipment and organic fertilizers as well as an extensive collection of fountains, sculptures, sundials and furniture

The Kinsman Company, Inc.
River Rd.
Point Pleasant, PA 18950
Tel: (215) 442–1740
Composting equipment and organic fertilizers, tools, rose arbors, garden arches and garden ornaments

Materials Unlimited
2 West Michigan Avenue
Ypsilanti, MI 48197
Tel: (313) 483–6980
Cast iron fences, posts, gates – catalog available

Moultrie Manufacturing Co.
P.O. Drawer 1179
Moultrie, GA 31768
Tel: (800) 841–8674
Fountains, metal fences, statuary, and furniture – catalog available

New England Garden Ornaments
38 East Brookfield Road
North Brookfield, MA 10535
Tel: (508) 867–4474
Agriframes, arches, gazebos, pergolas, tunnels, screens, topiary frames, and ornaments – catalog available

Resource Conservation Technology, Inc.
2633 North Calvert Street
Baltimore, MD 21218
Tel: (410) 366–1146
Rubber liners for garden ponds

Stone Forest
P.O. Box 2840
Santa Fe, NM 87504
Tel: (505) 986–8883
Fountains, stone basins, and hand-carved granite bird baths – catalog available

U.S. Bronze Powders, Inc.
Rt. 202, P.O. Box 31
Flemington, NJ 08822
Tel: (201) 782–5454
Metallic pigments and paints. For further information, send a self-addressed stamped envelope

Woodbrook
P.O. Box 175
Trussville, AL 35173
Tel: (800) 828–3607
Wooden garden furniture – catalog available

Woodcrafters
11840 N. U.S. 27
Dewitt, MI 48820
Woodcraft patterns: windmills, wishing wells, weather vanes, bird houses, whirligigs, jigsawing

CANADA
Cruikshanks Mail Order
Tel: 1-800-665-5605
Gardening supplies and accessories

Avant Gardener
2235 West 4th Avenue
Vancouver
British Columbia V6K 1N9
Tel: (604) 736-0404
Upscale garden accessories and garden statuary

Creative Wood Products
88 Shoemaker Street
Unit 1
Kitchener
Ontario N2E G4
Quality cedar furniture

Mason's Masonry Supply
6291 Netherhart Road
Mississauga
Ontario L5T 1A2
Paving supplies

INDEX

Page numbers in *italic* refer to the illustrations

accessories, 104–26, *104–27*
ageing:
    containers, 62–5
    sculpture, 110
aggregates, 24
alpine wheel, 27, *27*
alpines, 26, *26*
animals, 136, *136–7*
arbors, *61*, 82, *82*, *84–5*, 137
arches, *19*, *79–81*, 80, 82
atmosphere, 14
awnings, *128*, 132, *132*

bamboo canes, *124*
benches, 94, *94*
bird baths, *110*, 136, *137*
birds, 136
boundaries, 36
brick:
    edgings, 28
    floorings, *21–3*, 24, 25
    walls, 36–7, *36*
brushes, paint, 149, *149*
bucket, verdigris, 118, *118*
buildings, 86, *86–9*
bulbs, 18
butterflies, 136, *136*

cameo gardens, 72, *72–3*
candles, 140, *140–1*
canes, bamboo, *124*
canvas, deck chairs, 102–3, *102–3*
cast-iron furniture, *94*
chairs, 94, *95–7*, *101*, 130
chamomile lawns, 26
checkerboard patterns, *48*
chicken-box plant stand, 126, *126–7*
chicken-wire "cloche" 123, *123*
children's areas, 134, *134–5*
chimney, lead, 119, *119*
clay pots, 62–5, *62*, *65*
cleaning brushes, 149
climbing frames, 134, *135*
climbing plants, *16*, 37, *37*
"cloche", chicken-wire, 123, *123*
color, 18
    color-theme plantings, 52, *52–3*
    containers, 62–3, *62–3*
    furniture, 96, *96–7*
    paint, 46–7, *46–7*
    splash plantings, 70, *70–1*
concrete paving, 24, 25, 28

containers, *54*, 106
    cameo gardens, 72, *73*
    color, 18, 62–3, *62–3*
    color-theme plantings, 52
    decorating, 114, *114–15*
    gilded pots, 142, *142–3*
    hanging baskets, 66, *66–7*
    lead chimney, 119, *119*
    Mexican painted pots, 116, *116–17*
    miniature pond, *91*
    splash plantings, 70, *70–1*
    tin-can plant nursery, *74–5*
    verdigris bucket, 118, *118*
    window boxes, *63*, *68–9*

deck chairs, 101, 102–3, *102–3*
decking, 24, *24*
decorating brushes, 149, *149*
decorations, 106, *106–9*
    functional, 120, *120–3*
    table centerpieces, 146, *146–7*
dividers, 40, 80
doors, 42, *42–3*
dovecotes, *137*

edgings, 28, *28*
electricity:
    lighting, 138
    pumps, 90–1

entertaining, 144, *144*
entrances, 42, *42–3*

fences, 36, *36*, 37, *38*, 40, *40*, 46–7, *52*
flares, 140, *141*
floorings, 20–32, *20–33*
    decorative details, 32, *32*
    edgings, 28, *28*
    patterns, 29, *29*
focal points, 82, 110, *113*, 138
fountains, 90, 91
fragrance, 14, 130
functional decorations, 120, *120–3*
furniture, 94–102, *94–103*
    color, 96, *96–7*
    deck chairs, 101, 102–3, *102–3*
    garden console table, 100, *100*
    mosaic garden table, 98, *98–9*

garden console table, 100, *100*
gates, 42, *42*
gazebos, 86, *86–7*
gilded pots, 142, *142–3*

hammocks, 101, *101*
hanging baskets, 66, *66–7*
hearts:
    twig, 108, *108*
    wire, 108, *108–9*
hedges, 37, 40
herbs:
    cameo gardens, 72, *72*
    herb gardens, *22*
    herb lawns, 26

"Indian birds" design, 102
insects, 136
iron lantern, 145, *145*

knot gardens, 29

labels, *124*
lanterns, 140, *140–1*
    iron lantern, 145, *145*
lawns, 25, *25*
lead chimney, 119, *119*
levels, changing, 16, *16–17*, 25
lighting, 138–40, *138–41*
liners:
    hanging baskets, 66
    ponds, 91
living areas, 130, *130*
loungers, 101
love seats, 94

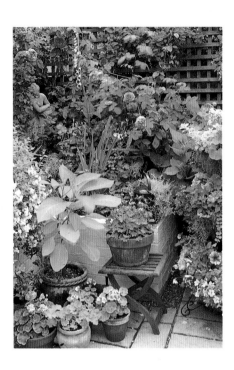

marbling, *49*
masonry, preparing surfaces, 150
metal, preparing surfaces, 151
Mexican painted pots, 116, *116–17*
miniature gardens, 72, *72*
miniature pond, *91*
mirrors, *110*
mosaics:
    on containers, *115*
    floors, 29
    miniature pebble circle, *33*
    mosaic garden table, 98, *98*
    pictures, *57*
    sculpture, 113

nightlights, 140, *141*

paint, 46–8, *46–51*, 148, *148*
    color, 46–7
    furniture, 96, *96–7*
    paint effects, 48, *48–9*
    preparing surfaces, 150–1
    tools, 149, *149*
parterres, 29, *29*
paths, edgings, 28, *28*
patterns, floors, 29, *29*
pea sticks, *124*
pebbles:
    floorings, 24
    miniature pebble circle, *33*
    mosaics, 29
    pretty pebble rug, 30, *30–1*
    water features, 91
pergolas, 12, 80, 82, *83*
perspective, 44, 80
picket fences, *36*, 40, *40*
pictures, 57, *57*
plant stands, *17*
    chicken-box plant stand, 126, *126–7*
plants, 58–76, *58–77*
    color-theme plantings, 52, *52–3*
    in hard surfaces, 26, *26*
    planning planting, 18, *18–19*
    as sculpture, 113
    splash plantings, 70, *70–1*
    table centerpieces, 146, *146–7*
playhouses, 10, 86, 88, *88–9*, 134, *134–5*
ponds, 90, *90–1*, 91
    miniature pond, *91*
potato prints, *48*
pots, 62–5, *62*, *65*
    decorating, 114, *114–15*
    gilded pots, 142, *142–3*
    Mexican painted pots, 116, *116–17*
preparing surfaces, 150–1
primers, 148
privacy, 12, *12*, 42, 44, 130

railings, 40, *40*
raised beds, *16*

romantic gardens, 14
rust bucket, 118
rustic poles, 40, *41*

sandpits, 10
scarecrows, *125*
scents, 14, 130
screens, 12, 40, 80, *80*, *129*, 130
sculpture, 106, 110–13, *110–13*, *125*, *137*
seedlings, tin-can plant nursery, *74–5*
sheds, *50–1*, 86, 92
shells:
    edgings, *28*
    wind chimes, 133, *133*
shelving, 54, 92, *92–3*
shingle, 24
slides, 134, *134*
splash plantings, 70, *70–1*
statues, 110, *113*
steamer chairs, 101
stencils, 48, *49*
    brushes, 149, *149*
    "stenciled-rug" design, 102–3, *103*
steps, 25, *25*
stippling, *49*, 149
stone:
    edgings, *28*
    floorings, 24, *24*, 25
    furniture, 94
    sculpture, 110
    stone-effect wall mask, *56*
storage, 92. *92–3*
structure, 18
sundials, *120*
supports:
    pea sticks, *124*
    twigwam, 122, *122*

table centerpieces, 146, *146–7*
tables, 94, 130, *130*
    garden console table, 100, *100*
    mosaic garden table, 98, *98–9*
terracotta pots, 62–5, *62*, *65*, 114, *114*
    gilded pots, 142, *142–3*
textures, 14, 130
thyme:
    cameo gardens, 72, *72*
    grass, 26
tiles:
    edgings, *28*
    panels, *34*, 57, *57*
    patterns, 29, *29*
timber:
    decking, 24, *24*
    fences, 40
    preparing surfaces, 150–1
tin-can plant nursery, *74–5*
toads, 136
tools:
    as decorations, 120, *120*

painting, 149, *149*
topiary, 37, 76, *76*, 113, *113*
tree houses, 134
trees, 18
trellis, 12, 37, *37*, 40, *41*, 44, *44–5*, 80, *80*, *84–5*, 129
trompe l'oeil, 48, *49*
twigs:
    hearts, 108, *108*
    twigwam, 122, *122*

umbrellas, 132, *132*
urns, 106

vegetable gardens, 124, *124–5*
verdigris bucket, 118, *118*
vistas, *129*, 130

walkways, *79*, 82, *83*
wall mask, stone-effect, *56*
walls, 34
    boundaries, 36–7
    decorations, 54, *54–7*
water features, *15*, 90–1, *90–1*, 110, 130
watering cans, 120, *121*
wattle fencing, 37, *38*
wildlife, 136, *136–7*
windbreaks, 132
wind chimes, 133, *133*
window boxes, *63*, *68–9*
wire, hearts, 108, *108–9*
wood:
    decking, 24, *24*
    fences, 40
    preparing surfaces, 150–1
wood stains, 150–1
wrought-iron furniture, *94*

ACKNOWLEDGMENTS

My thanks:

To *Debbie*, whose wonderful evocative photographs so brilliantly capture the very essence of "the decorated garden room", and for sharing with me an incredibly busy summer.

To all the contributors whose varied skills, creativity, and talent have enriched the project element of the book.

To all the people who so generously let us photograph in their gardens, and whose infectious enthusiasm for gardening has enriched the design and plant element of the book.

To *Judith*, for coming back from maternity leave and so quickly grasping the character of the book, then guiding it into production.

To *Maggie Daykin* for being such a swift, sensitive and brilliant editor.

To *Lisa Tai*, designer, for bringing it all so beautifully to fruition.

And finally . . . to *Richard*, *Zoe* and *Faye* for being so patient through the summer in a house looking like a cross between a garden center and home improvement store, and *Debby*, *Christein* and *Mijke* who entertained the children while I gathered the material for the book.

CONTRIBUTORS

Cleo Mussi
Alpine Wheel, Miniature Pebble Circle, Pretty Pebble Rub and Mosaic Garden Table projects.

Liz Wagstaff
Decorating a Shed, Stone-effect Wall Mask, Garden Console, Lead Chimney, Verdigris Bucket, Gilded Pots and Iron Lantern projects.

Karin Hossack
Tin-can Plant Nursery, Twigwam, Mexican Painted Pots, Chicken Box Plant Stand and Windchime projects, and the plant label plaque featured on page 124.

Jenny Norton
Painting the Customized Play House, painting the chairs on pages 96 and 97 and painting the wall featured on page 47.

Mijke Gesthuizen
Wire Heart project.

LOCATIONS

With many thanks to the following people, who very kindly let us photograph their gardens:
Bryan d'Alberg, Bill Blake and his gardener, Julian Hobbs, John Casson, Countess of Chichester, Mr and Mrs Eadie, Lucinda Ganderton, Ivan and Angela Hicks at The Garden in the Mind, Stanstead Park, Sandra Hanauer, Tony Hills at Wallace Antiques and Art, Cuckfield, Sheila Jackson, Ann Kennedy of Agriframes, East Grinstead, Lady Anne Rasch at Heale House Gardens, Diana Ross, Drummond Shaw of Drummonds of Bramley, and Gay Wilson.